The ADVANTAGE OF A HANDICAP

TWELVE SERMONS BY
M. S. RICE

THE ABINGDON PRESS
NEW YORK   CINCINNATI

TO
LAURA BUCKNER RICE
DAUGHTER
WIFE
MOTHER
OF METHODIST PREACHERS

CONTENTS

FOREWORD

THE preacher, who can never know his audience, can never prepare his sermon for those who are there, and hence what he says, if it must forever remain no more than said, may fail of the destination to which it carries most meaningful message. For that reason these sermons, unrelated to each other, and selected to cover a scattered range of interest, are committed to type. It is the hope of the preacher that the ministry of the spoken word may, by the assistance of the printed word, make preaching a bit more permanent.

M. S. R.

DETROIT, 1924.

I

THE ADVANTAGE OF A HANDICAP

"The lame take the prey."—Isa. 33. 23.

THAT strange clause caught my attention as religiously significant, because so very humanly unusual. I have frequently found God at work where human logic seemed to be avoided. The lame is not qualified to take the prey in ordinary. We train our proud and strong bodies for the struggle. We place confidence in strength. We feel sure of the value of the swift foot rather than the hobbling step. If we are to win, we fortify ourselves with what we call readiness. We ordinarily pity the lame. We catch our best interpretation of our own strength at times when we make bold to offer to supplement the handicap of some other, and fancy thus we have but shown our own abundant endowment; for we did not expect to lose our own case, but only to apply the extra strength we were sure we possessed.

The lame, oh, the lame!—we cannot think in such terms to find victory. God frequently writes religious truth in terms contrary to human reckoning. He sometimes has to dismiss a whole army, and disarm even the remaining few, and give them mere pitchers to hold, in order to show men how he works. He sometimes is compelled to hand his servant a small stick, with which to break a great rock in Horeb, just to keep him convinced that it is God who is working. All down a long story the same truth is worked out in multiplied ways that men may appreciate that when God works it frequently becomes necessary to destroy the foundation of human confidence. Proud human strength may be left to stand unaided in the strength it is so sure of. The very best expression of human conduct has been written in the fact that the lame, because of their handicap, have been made partakers of the strength of others, and such a challenge has not infrequently brought to strength itself the supernatural help which lurks in the genuine fact of unselfish devotion. When the great ship staggered at sea, wounded by the lurking peril that awaited her destruction, and the waters of doom began to creep up on her settling sides, the cry rang out, "Women and children first," and the real strength of manhood, challenged in the fact that the weaker ones had no chance in themselves, was shown, not because it was able to hurl aside every timid woman, and shrinking child, and clamber into the lifeboats for rescue. No, no! The strength of strength was shown in that it could stand back and graciously assist with strong hands the weaker ones into the lifeboats. The strong were strong only as they were able to control their strength. They found their own victory only as in unselfish administration of what could have been a triumph of selfishness, they gave way to weakness.

Maybe in oft-hurried reading of the Bible you have read carelessly past this text clause, without catching its concealed significance. It is a truly beautiful way of saying that God keeps watch over his creation and maintains a strange balance there. There certainly obtains a profound compensation in the equipment of nature. There is not an equal endowment in aggressive strength, but nevertheless God's solicitous care is bestowed upon all. It is a wonderful sentiment, and very like God in its declaration, that he has with infinite care looked upon everything, and has supplemented the natural weakness of some with an ofttimes confounding measure of strength. "The lame take the prey," sounding when I first read it as a strange declaration that lacked truth in utterance, and framed in unreasonable sentiment only, seems upon more careful consideration, to be a clear loving evidence of exactly what I had expected of the God of us all. It is refreshingly satisfactory as evidence of his providence.

The world has always built its confidence with such ease upon its strength. We have learned to stand up close beside the evidence we could gather and talk of preparedness. We mean by such a word (that has come to great respect in such an iron-cannoned, gun-powdered, steel-plated day as this is) that we have gathered every recognized strong thing that can be gathered, and are, by comparison with others, able to care for ourselves. Care for ourselves! How? By pounding someone who is not quite able to pound us.

How does such talk sound when measured beside the rights of those who are weak and cannot carry as big a gun as can we? The world's confidence just now is in strength. Sixteen-inch cannon! How strangely satisfactory their long, gleaming barrels do seem, and how commandingly their great black, round mouths seem to speak! Soldiers! Enlist them down rows of millions. They must be physically fit. Only the best man! You cannot limp and be enlisted. Out of the way, ye lame! The right of might demands armies of ablest-bodied men for battle. Back from the fields out there, where they will blast out victory, they will likewise send us great droves of broken, maimed, hobbling, fragmented bodies. The lame will come staggering home as contribution to the harder tasks of peace. Out of the way, ye lame!—the cry of a war-crazed world.

We have, however, even with our fierce wreckage of human bodies, at least advanced as a world to a point where we do pity the lame. We used to kick them out of the road, maybe the very road they found their lameness by defending. But to-day we are at least careful toward them. The wounded wring our hearts with pity, and I have seen great throngs lift their hats and cheer as the wounded heroes went hobbling by.

No one, but God, however, would ever have imagined lameness to be an equipment. Who but God would ever dare declare that the man who goes forth accoutered with lameness carries thus the weapons of conquest? "The lame take the prey." Compensation does not fail. The law evolves in nature the very thing that seems lacking. One of the most interesting evident facts of life is the oft-seen triumph of those who, though endowed with but little, have seemed able to work that little with extreme success, while all about them were those who though flushed with opportunity and endowment have been prodigal with their strength and scattered it even unto poverty, without sense of economy. "The survival of the fittest" is a phrase that has become a veritable "billy club" of investigation to-day. I am awaiting a full specification as to just what the fittest means. We are faced with some strange survivals. Microbes must be reckoned with. They seem to be comers. Little sign of their dying off. They have no friends. Their enemies are legion. They survive. Did you ever consider what giants those were whose skeletons the eager geologists are digging up here and there across our earth to-day, and building into such colossal forms in our museums we can scarce find rooms to house them? Extinct beasts these. Mammoths and many other large monsters we have found, since in our dull ignorance we used the biggest word we had on what we thought the largest of them all. Dead and gone. Survival of the fittest? Who will define for us now, faced as we are by such strange survivals and such strange extinctions, what fitness really is?

There is another deeply searching passage of Scripture quite closely related here, "To them that have no might he increaseth strength." The smallest and most delicate things that live are endowed with strange ability. Delicate animals, and birds, know how to enlist the strength of nature about them, and thus to hide their own defenselessness in the might of something else. Where is the boy who has known a boy's right of living afield, who has not been outwitted by the tiny quail whose covey he startled? Those little brown things know exactly how to hide. I have found little lizards hiding on the rocks or in the grass: brown with the rocks, green with the grass. The rabbits of the north woods turn white when winter comes, and thus enlist the very mantle of winter to compensate their weakness. The fleet hare of our Western prairies, confident of his swift feet, seeks the open country where he can run. The little common rabbit stays near the brush heaps and bushes and rocks, from whose help he can enlist aid. I was driving along a country lane one afternoon, and a great brown falcon hawk whirled past my head with a sound like a strong wind. It startled me to look quickly and see running for a dense thicket of wild roses a frightened and hurrying rabbit. The hawk struck him, just as he reached the bushes, and got only the last arriving section of that rabbit, which isn't much. The thicket saved him. God's word for it, "The conies are but a feeble folk, yet make they their houses in the rocks." The very rocks fight for their weakness.

In this universe of God's, marked all over, as it is, with eloquent evidence of his care, there is evident a law which makes up the very thing which seems to be lacking. The advantage of

the handicap is a hopeful religious fact. I am
sure an honest, unselfish study of any life will
bear undeniable testimony of its remembrance
of God. God is in this world. His hand is upon
our affairs. Somehow he does overbalance all
seeming evil by great benefit. This is God's
world. Of course I realize how poorly we understand it. I know how it has often seemed that
truth was on the scaffold and wrong was on
the throne. Yet, if we have but carefully sat
before that scaffold and throne, we have been
compelled to reach the poet's familiar conclusion which stands unshaken beyond such mere
facts as scaffolds and thrones. In a careless
world scaffold and throne would almost seem
like conclusions. But they are not. God stands
within the shadows. This is the wholesome,
undeniable doctrine of Christian optimism
taught so unquestioningly by Paul, when he
declared, "All things work together for good to
them that love God." The lame actually do take
the prey. It is eloquent in life everywhere.

Did you ever try to analyze for explanation
the forces which entered into the make-up of the
most beautiful lives you have ever known! I
have frequently tried to do it just to confirm
the faith I hold. The evolution of the character
of Jacob, which brought him out of the poor life
he once lived in self-centered bargain-making,

and made of him one of the characters upon
whom long history could be hung, is interesting.
He wrestled with an angel all a long night in
the confidence of his own strength. Toward
morning the angel touched his thigh and left him
a lame man, and by that, thrust him into the
position of his triumph, and made possible the
victory he won by simply clinging, a lame man,
to his antagonist. Thenceforth Jacob limping
on his hard way down the road where his cara-
van of camels and goats and cattle had gone,
came into his greatest victory.

The destiny of humanity is a large program.
That part you and I have to play in it here on
this earth for a few years, doubtless will matter
but little. I am but one, and one of the least, in
the great race. I cannot see the truth of even
my life, though, if I bound it by the narrow walls
of my own sorrow, or of my own enjoyment.

The lameness of the lame must not monopolize
his attention. That has been the chief trouble
with the lame. His imperfections have been the
center of his consciousness. He has asked pity
because he was lame. He has asked help because
he was lame. Thus the interpretation and
expression of his life have been around and out
of the fact of his impediment. Many rich and
strong things have been compelled to lie dormant
in his life while he has exhibited his imperfec-

tions. He has forgotten what he has had, in the glaring sense of what he has not had. Recently it was my privilege to be in attendance at a large banquet of business men, at which the guest of honor was brought in after we had all found our places. He was wheeled to his place at the center of the speakers' table, a mere fragment of a human body. From his neck down he was a complete wreck. He had been so from birth. His father and mother had wished and actually prayed that he might die. There he was in that banquet, a man of large business enterprise. He had made himself rich and influential, by making use, not of the imperfections, of which he had so many, but of the powers he still possessed. He thrilled us all with the address he delivered and sent every one of us out of the room determined to use life as it had been given us.

Josiah Wedgwood was a lame, uneducated, and neglected potter boy. Everything gathered about him to discourage his soul. But he exalted his trade till his very name is flavored with the sense of fine art. He has hung lovely medallions on the walls of a whole world whose certification of value is in the mere name Wedgwood.

Shall my lameness dominate me! Shall I hush my song on lips determined to be mute, because my eyes have lost their luster? Shall I put the scepter of rulership into the hands of my calam-

ity, and subject all the rest of my life to the
tyranny of my disability? Or shall I rather,
as rare and inspirational Helen Keller did, whet
the sense I have left on the calamity of all those
I have lost, and thus conquer a greater battle
than would have ever been offered me had I gone
perfect into the conflict? Had Helen Keller come
on into life, even a brilliant girl, though with
physical perfection, she might never have been
heard of outside her own little circle. As it is
her name has run to the ends of the world and
will be an inspiration to encouragement forever.

I shall not despair because some fierce blows
may have fallen upon me. The whole process of
this world is to take from, and not add to.
Michael Angelo never added to the marble. He
cut it away. He answered his critic one day,
"Yes, the marble is wasted, but the angel grows."
Mere marble blocks! Any rough quarryman
with a stick of dynamite can blast out marble
chunks. I was recently over a railroad track
through a portion of Lake Champlain, built on
great tumbled-in blocks of Vermont marble. If
some Angelo could come that way and strike
from one block I saw there all the hindering and
concealing bulk of the stone, and disconceal a
masterpiece, that railroad would halt the traffic
till the treasure could be rescued and placed on
a pedestal of appreciation some great where.

God knows what he is doing in this world. I shall not criticize the chips that sometimes fall blinding upon my face, and litter the path about my feet. But I shall, the rather, pray for grace to realize that the blow I may receive is not an end of the design toward me, but, rather only the process by which the design shall be perfected. If I can but get myself thoroughly grounded thus, I can then face all the problems of my loneness. God has forgotten nothing, nor has he forgotten me. The doctrine of his providence is that in the places of our greatest exposure shall be revealed the scenes of our most signal deliverances. Even aside from the sacred story, and in the paths where ordinary heroism has turned blood-red in the way of truth, we have seen souls strangely upborne. When they have limped their way they have caught step with victory. Hell never draws near to a soul, but heaven comes too, and lures with secret constraints toward its secure pathways. Could I but lay bare the whole life of even the humblest and most obscure individual within our acquaintance, we would discover the eloquent truth that "He giveth power to the faint; and to them that have no might he increaseth strength." Out of stony griefs across all the ways life has had to come, mankind has been forever raising Bethels.

All this leads us surely into the peace that

comes from profound confidence in God. There is no finer chapter yet written in the human story than the one on confidence in God written around the experiences of handicapped lives. God will balance our lives. Doubtless one of the most widely known and fiercest sentences ever pronounced in this world was the word of Anne of Austria to Richelieu. "My Lord Cardinal," said she, "God does not pay at the end of every week; but at the end he pays." All that is as true for mercy and reward as it is for justice, and must be heard in its whole meaning. Horace Bushnell has onewhere a remarkable passage in which he is arguing for the constructive value of difficulty. He seeks to extract the dangers from every hard thing; to take the heat out of fire, and the cold out of frost, and the shock out of the lightning, and the roar out of the thunder. It is a brilliant attempt to raise a man before a world such as this is, with all its attendant danger removed, and there to face such a coddled creature as he would be with the genuine issues human life must draw. Jacob must have his thigh thrown out, and go on lame to the greatness of which he was capable. He could limp his way to victory. He never could have walked proudly erect to possess it. "The lame take the prey." Measure your life to that fact. When once the lame catch heart beyond their lameness they begin to gain strength to conquer. There are many souls among us who by unusual privileges and endowed with rare ability seem surely equipped for highest service, and yet they are not weighing an ounce in the great spiritual work that waits to be done. There are others who, crippled and hindered by serious restrictions, are still genuine factors of service. Browning has written it in most fascinating manner in the ministry unconscious but real, of a wonderful but handicapped soul, in the story of "Pippa Passes." It is the resolute will and the unconquerable heart that win; and such spirit will win even though every energy seems to be embarrassed and crippled by genuinely perplexing restrictions.

I was walking through the hall of a lovely home one day and saw on the floor, beside beautiful rugs and amid costly draperies, a rough chunk of a broken rock. I thought as I saw it first that it had found its place only by the insistence of sentiment. Maybe it was a fragment of a dear old homestead. Maybe it had come from some famous place. There must be some hidden reason for a rough, unfinished stone to have been given a place in a mansion. As I passed by and dared to cast one more wondering glance at that strange thing as I thought, I beheld the secret of it all. A genius for sure had been at that rock. Leaving the rough exterior just as the ill-shaped thing had come to his hands, he had carved back into one side of it a rarely beautiful face. So tenderly graceful and fine did it seem, as it looked out from that rough, unhewn stone, that I have remembered it as distinct among the many faces I have seen rescued from hindering stone by hands of genius. I have been carrying that artist's setting of beauty against my life ever since. How often do great rough challenges come up before me. I am not to bewail and criticize the handicaps that may be upon me. I pray God to help me carve out of them somehow the fine contribution of genuine compensation. The greatest thing that can happen to a human life is not to be set free from handicap. I am lame! Oh I am lame! My God, hear my cry and heal this hurt of mine! How easily such cries leap to our lips in prayer! Yet I cannot see the fact of God to me as other than at times in preservation of my distress, so called, and even in redirection of it for truer service. Lame man, your lameness may be your strength.

Some time ago a very wonderful word was flung at the world by a daring and determined man, who was setting himself to a task so hard, he knew it would try the courage of those he left behind him, to keep faith with his endeavor long enough to let him have the extreme chance

of victory.   Stefansson set sail into the North.
When the very last place from which any word
could be sent back to the world had been reached,
and the only word that would ever again be
heard from them would be a returning shout, or
the delayed discovery of their fate in failure,
that rugged explorer chose this great final sentence, "Do not rescue us prematurely."   How
that fine appeal in daring fairly flaunts heroism
at us!   We know the bite of frost!   We know
the peril of hunger!   We know the burden of the
persistent darkness!   We know the dull weight
of the monotonous endurance!   We know!   We
know!   But don't rescue us prematurely!   We
have come out here to endure and conquer.   "The
lame take the prey."

> "Behold we know not anything,
>   I can but trust that good shall fall,
>   At last, far off, at last to all,
> And every winter change to spring."

II

WHO GIVES HIMSELF

"Hereby perceive we the love of God, because he laid down his life for us: and we ought to lay down our lives for the brethren."—1 John 3. 16.

THE effectual disposal of life, with all its manifold wealth, is our prime problem in investment. The passion of the world at present, is not expended upon how it can best give itself. Life seems just now to be more studiously concerned as to how it can most effectually collect for itself.

The incident, which has precipitated in my thought the interpretation I am daring to put here against one of the most sacred sentences in the Bible, may sound at first mention somewhat coarse, and of light meaning. It is to me, however, everything else, and I am hoping I may be able to interpret it to you in the impressive manner in which it came into my experience. If it shall be separated from the involved meaning here, it will be utterly misunderstood, and doubtless become to me a point for severe criticism. This incident, separated from the line of my

27

contention, was printed in an Eastern paper recently and immediately started the ever ready newspaper correspondent who drew conclusions utterly amiss, because he could see in it nothing but an argument in finance.

A man, who was genuinely concerned over the higher calls of Christianity came to see me one day with troubled soul, because of a questioning objection that had been raised to him by one who saw but one side of cost. He had been talking to his friend about joining the church, and was encouraged to it. When he mentioned the fact that the church he had in mind to join was the church of which I am the preacher, his friend, knowing we were engaged in a large building enterprise, advised him against his intention and used these words, "Don't join that church; they will soak you." That troubled the troubled man, even more. It was a weaving of finance into a problem where finance has no prime place. The troubled man, however, refused to dismiss his interest so cheaply, and decided to come personally to see me about it. He told me the whole incident. When he had finished, I looked him straight in the face and replied: "Your friend was right. We will 'soak' you. If you are afraid of being 'soaked,' don't join here. If you are looking for a cheap church, don't join this church. Go somewhere

else, and may God help the cheap door you enter
in his name."

The man saw the challenge in the great outstanding fact, that has written the story of
religion all across the world in the reddest blood
of sacrifice, and said, I am sure I caught the
sense of eagerness in his saying, "You may take
my name!"

I have been glad, many, many times, because
that incident came to my experience. There is
not the faintest expression of money in it. It
breathes the real meaning of the espousal of the
faith that has written sacrifice in terms, even of
God himself, into this world's life. His church
cannot stand in any less costly way in its appeal
to its devotees!

"That church will soak you!" Thank God for
the reputation. The more I thought of the
warning the more I favored the church therefor.
I was sure it was the church I was hunting. I
wouldn't belong to a church that didn't "soak"
me. I would be afraid of drying up. Christianity will "soak" you. Thank God for that.
After all there is very little in this world that is
any more essential to your true conduct than
that. I would stand in the pulpit of his great
church, and call the fact straight to your souls.
I am stirred to deepest conviction, with the call
of the obligated sacrifice of life.

We cannot sit under the glowing example of our Lord's great sacrifice of himself, and fail to feel the conclusion his great friend and apostle wrote here, that we ought also to lay down our lives for the brethren. Are you looking now for a comfortable place, in this badly broken world in the greatest crisis of its whole history thus far, where you can find a shelter from cost, and where there will be no conscription that will send you far beyond any feeling of ease? If you are, then the Church of Jesus Christ is no place for you to turn in.

What was it that made the Great War at its very worst moments an irresistible challenge to strong, courageous youth, and sent them in solid phalanx running out to meet it? Was it a carefully arranged escape from hardship and cost, and an avoidance of all those things we call sacrifice? Was it because they thought they had found a favored seat where they could in undisturbed indulgence sip their sparkling glasses of pleasure, and let the world go by? Was it an offered shelter from flying shells, and the smell of death? Oh no! Every one of us has to remember that, in mad days when hatred and destruction get the call, and can find an interpretation in the terms of genuine sacrifice, then it is sure to catch the ears of eager youth, and they turn not back from any campaigning.

Afraid you will get "soaked!" You are not afraid of that if you have found the right adjustment of heart and soul. The unalterable fact of life, anyhow, is, that in one way or in another you must pay up. None of us will ever be able to get through this life by beating that required collection. No one else is going to pay your obligation in this world. The lineage of the dodger is a very short line here. Someone once asked a great professor, why it was always spoken about God's judgments as being visited upon the third and fourth generations only, thus leaving the twelfth and all the rest untouched. "Because," answered the wise man in fine conclusion, "there is no seventh generation in evil. Four is as far as it can stumble on."

I realize full well, that I have made use of rough phraseology to build up an approach to the consideration of the most divinely interpreted fact of life's indebtedness I know anything about. The apostle John makes so bold as to dare to link this appeal to the very finest expression of the ways of God himself. "Hereby perceive we the love of God, because he laid down his life for us: and we ought to lay down our lives for the brethren." There cannot be laid against that word any accusation of hunting ease. It sounds almost too bold, and were it not plain written here in the Bible, none of us with pens that carried no claim on inspiration would dare pen such words. Daring to measure the obligations of men beside the sacrifice of Jesus Christ, the altogether unapproachable event this earth has ever had enacted upon it, and standing before it we conclude there can be no human escape from supreme cost. Can it be possible that I shall ever again hear anyone say, in seeking an affiliation with the church that is founded on a Saviour's love, that it is too costly! Can I ever find a word that could express what its cost to me could mean? It killed Him. It surely ought to crush the very souls out of a very great many more of us, and brush forever from our lips any small words of cheap complaint.

To the heroism of the great Christian espousal I would call you now. There was a sacrifice in the old church Jesus came to change. That old church kept a bloody altar where the bright crimson was spilled from lambs that were unwillingly dragged to the slaughter. To the sacrifice itself, then, the altar was no better than a slaughter house; and from his standpoint, sacrifice was a hideous death run red before a gleaming knife that could not be dodged. The weak was the victim. Jesus Christ introduced a new element in sacrifice. He himself is the sacrifice. The offerer himself became the offering. The volunteer in sacrifice has changed the whole service. Sacrifice now has won its own case, because of the worth of the offering itself. Jesus Christ, Son of God, the first great evidence. The weak for the strong, was the long, long story written across centuries of bloody altars. While the strong may have, in their deep intentions, found some virtue by that service, it was all found in the sacrificer who stood with the knife. Weakness was the victim. Why? For just one reason: it was not strong enough to victimize another, or to force its own frightened escape. Weakness! Poor little trembling doves and lambs, frightened at the smell of blood. When they died it was merely death. When Jesus Christ, strong Son of God, came to tread the path of sacrifice, he wrote death into sacrifice in such terms that the world can never again think of it merely in terms of a victim. There is a fine and overwhelming sense of indebtedness we all feel at our best moments, when we really catch the full interpretation of our ability as our responsibility. What our day awaits now in most eager need toward the people of God who have the real welfare of the world at heart, is for us all to find our own honest places, and there absolutely burn our lives to the socket in service.

Of course that will "soak" you! You ought to get "soaked." That's the very genius of Christianity. "The survival of the fittest," is a phrase that has been spoken in a confident inflection about the earth of late days, as though it were very high, as well as very scientific talk. It has assumed a presumption in scholasticism. I cannot agree that it is very high talk, no matter how scholastic it may be. It is a law that has been evolved out of the lowest of life. It has been interpreted around the lives of microbes and beasts. I must confess to a positive lack of enthusiasm, over any arguments for conduct of my own life, based upon the actions of lions and tigers, and the bleeding story of mere surviving. As a man I ask for a better rule. I would lift my head to a higher way. I was reading one of the recent books, where the author has been arguing for a more fierce practicality in life, a book quite widely read too, in which this passage occurs: "Civilization has wrought some profound changes, the most important of which is a modification of the natural process of selection for survival. So long as man was a savage, or even a barbarian, nature continued to select, virtually unhindered, according to her ancient plan, eliminating the weak and preserving the strong. But civilization meant a change, from a natural to a more or less artificial, man-made environment, in which natural selection was increasingly modified by social selection, and social selection altered survival values, all along the line."[1] Of course the author argued that way merely to show how civilization was breaking down by overburdening the strong with the weak. He was endeavoring to get a release into selfish expression, for the strong of the world. It is a new announcement of an argument Goethe made use of some time ago.

We will not surrender the great altruistic stride that has come into interpretation of human conduct under the teaching and leadership of our great Master, merely because it will impose heavy burdens upon the strong. Let the strong bear the burden of the weak, has better authority, and more inspirational challenge to human life than talk about the survival of the fittest. Maybe surviving is not a fair judgment. I know some of the very greatest who didn't survive, and, indeed, who quit surviving, because they were in pursuit of bigger business. I cannot find words in my better vocabulary that will be uttered in protest against the thought. The really great fact must remain, as eloquent as any fact that has ever been brought into the demonstration of living, that all the great achievements of righteousness in the world, have come about when we have seen the complete

---

[1] Stoddard, *Revolt Against Civilization.* Used by permission of Charles Scribner's Sons, New York.

reversal of the mere physical law of evolution. We have walked most like humans, when might has voluntarily made of itself a sacrifice. When that voluntary element has appeared in sacrifice, it has at once put into it more than death. It has made that death in itself indicative. It has called our attention to the purpose of its service.

When Thoreau wrote about life in such a meaning, he used that biting comment about the hanging of John Brown, "He could not get even a vote of thanks, or a pair of boots for his life. He could not get four and six pence a day for being hung the year round." It was not death that was being sold. It was not death that John Brown was offering on the world's altar then. More than death was there. Little did John Brown care for what he was to get there. It was never in the contract. It never can be written into that contract by an ever so ill-balanced judgment of life. He was there, the sacrifice himself. He was therefore there with the highest motive. Thoreau insisted there was a better price for a quart of milk than for a quart of blood in the market place at Concord. But that does not enter the argument, for heroes do not bring their blood to the market. Where is that man now who is afraid of being "soaked"! The blood of the truly great of this world's real

doing, has never been paid for, and never can
be paid for. Pay is too coarse talk to bring into
their presence. The great, strong, noble, pure,
of this world! those who have made our race
wear the name "human" with more apparent fitness, have not been paid for the offering they
made. Not by riches, nor by fame, nor by power,
nor by anything else that man could offer at his
counter, but only by the fullness of their God-
struck lives have they found any reward for their
service.

Where has this greatest truth for life ever had
such conclusive setting as it has had in Christianity? Where were you ever offered so noble
an opportunity of escape from all that is little,
and selfish, and mean, as you have been offered
in the big program of the church of Christ?
Who has ever imagined a measure of this great
truth so perfect, as that which our Lord and
Saviour has wrought out to eloquent conclusion,
in the life he lived, and the God-acknowledged
death he died? Who, beside, on this earth has
ever come nearer to that, than the noble self-
sacrificing men and women, who, professing his
name, have actually thrown their lives before
every phase of need among men, and have will-
ingly given their substance to keep up the work!
I contend that Christianity is the creature of
this great truth. Our religion lives by the prac-

tice of this fact. It is the open secret of all the success we have ever had. It is the strongest appeal we have made to the world. It is the outstanding distinction that marks and will mark our chief characters. The story of the church is the story of those who have been absolutely supreme in service. Those who have effectually laid life down. Keep away from the Christian Church, for it will "soak" you. It will. But by the very act of "soaking" you it will likewise save you from the dry-rot of your own dead selfishness.

There stands the impressive character of that martyred hero, Paul from Tarsus. How stands he before the world? Is he on a pedestal of careful self-service? Did he get off easy? Were there roses strewn along his way? You cannot think of him separated from the struggle. His whole story has been written in persecution and suffering, as he insisted on bestowing himself upon the world in need under the controlling sense of his own indebtedness. Paul would have gone down and been buried in black oblivion under the dead multitude about him had he been controlled by so little a fear as the cost of it all. "I am debtor! I am debtor!"—so cried he, as he went everywhere seeking to discharge his obligation, and ever conscious of the fact that it would never be paid until he had actually bestowed all he could be upon a world that needs every man's best laid upon the great altar, to help the whole world heavenward.

It was at that very point where the rich young ruler made his pathetic failure in life. Jesus brought him squarely before this fact. He saw, across the years, what that fine young fellow could become. He told him plainly how to do it. "What shall I do, Lord?" The Master answered clearly: "Go sell your goods! Give your riches away, and come and follow me!" That halting, slinking, young man was the early example of the one who feared the church would "soak" him. He refused. "You don't catch me with such an expensive program," was the confident word he answered. He went away with every bit of his money. He never dropped a penny even. He saved all he had. But that was all.

What a truth this, for our day! This day of big fortunes. This day of distinguishable few. This day of easy-going strength. What a truth this is, with which to strike deep into the heart of ability! Oh for the preacher to arise who can put eloquence into so significant a message, and make it into a conviction! Your blood! Your blood! Not on the battlefield. Not in the market place. Your blood on the world's altar. There is no money on that altar for you. But who would

sell blood for lucre? We ask you for sacrifice.
Your power is your debt. Whatever you are,
you owe. You should be "soaked." It is the
very need of life. You cannot make out your
life on easier terms. You are a slave without it.
Christ's life and death are the supreme eloquence
of the fact. We can never dare permit a cry at
our lips on so poor a level as this slang phrase
we have been trying to drive the slang from, in
the interpretation of the tragic blunder in its
suggestion, when once we see Jesus Christ. The
very price of being a man or a woman of genuine
strength in this world is that we shall be of
actual service. Power is debt. Every power
must be interpreted in obligation. Of course the
severe temptation of power is now, and has
always been, to sit aside in its own high place,
and charge the world toll. The tragedy—or I
suppose comedy would be a better word—of
power has been its servants. Power has always
been recipient. The man who needs servants is
the weak man. He needs care at the point of his
weakness. A man has not begun to breathe the
real sense of his power, until he has caught the
sense of an overpowering moral indebtedness.
His greatness has not taken root in appreciation
of itself, until it recognizes in itself a power to
help and better the world. He cannot even find
footroom for his influence while he is enamored

of cold selfishness, and hears in every call of a
world's need merely a design to "soak" him
again. We only begin to walk as men and women
in Christian bearing when we feel that a contribution is asked of us, to the invisible interests of the universe. We are actually here to
add something to the world's spiritual assets.
Oh, that each of us now, could see life holding
out its empty palms in solicitation! You are
not here to collect your dues. You are here to
pay your bills. All humanity has claim upon
you. You cannot shake it off. You cannot dodge
it. "No man liveth to himself," and God means
that the real conviction of that fact shall work
itself out then in the question of finer imputa-
tion: To whom, then, do I live? "We ought to
lay down our lives for the brethren," so con-
cludes the apostle John, under the spell of close
association with Jesus. "For their sakes I sanctify myself"—so declares our Lord as he looked
down the ages of need. That is the sure obligation upon the Christian. It is the impulse that
will carry our lives out, through, and triumph-
antly beyond whatever demands of service may
come appealingly. With that interpretation we
will not chafe under the insistent request for
help, nor think we have been "soaked," because
we shall have been enlisted in sacrifice. We will,
the rather, give welcome to every possible

expenditure of ourselves, and of our ability in the way of true service.

The church will "soak" you! Yes, sir, it will, if it can but get life correctly before you. That is exactly what you need. None of us have need of the lavishing of every spare dollar we can obtain, just to be able to say at last that we have had a good time. Every one of us does need to find the clear road to devotion, and there to lay down our lives in dedication to service.

Who gives himself? Oh that strong souls would hear the call! Let rich men and women hear it. Let cultured men and women hear it. Let young men and women hear it. Culture, knowledge, riches, taste, practical skill—any form of power, is impaired and perverted to the degree in which it misses the element of ministry, and looks upon life here as an opportunity to collect a debt. The world is creditor, not you. You are bound to be "soaked."

The whole world in its halting progress waits for obligation to become a passion among the strong. This thing has arisen to a clamor in my ears these days. I am not senseless of the splendid service many are rendering. I am only lashed of soul by the fact of those who do not respond. The price of blood is upon this. We ought to lay down our lives. Under the leadership of such a call, we will never be troubled with so shallow a question as to whether or no life is worth living. Who ever originated that pessimistic question anyhow? It was never asked by Paul. It was not asked by Luther. It was never asked by any man or woman, who, ablaze with interest, brought life up to a white-heat of participant endeavor. Such a question was duly prompted in the bloom of some idler's heart, who, sitting with condemned hands in his do-nothing lap, and thinking in selfishness of some dawdling ease soon spent in its own indulgence, looked up and asked as it lazily yawned in conscious uselessness, "Is life worth living?"

Who gives himself? There is no other way for the really great service to be rendered. It cannot be paid for. At the best you will get "soaked." It is only in that unpurchasable consciousness of duty that attends true sacrifice, that any reward can possibly accrue. No man or woman was ever paid for being burned at the stake, or chained to choke in the rising tide. The thought of pay in such association is insulting to our best sense of obligation.

Come with me yonder to that quiet, lovely little town among the hills at Harper's Ferry, and stand on that strange day among us nationally, that we have never yet been able to find words to describe. They come leading out a strange son of the West, who was born in the East, and go toward a rough scaffold there. He walks with remarkable confidence. He was a bit rough in his way, but his was a rough way. A strange crowd lined his last pathway, but there were no stranger ones there than he who went to death. Just as the hangman reaches to pull the trap beneath his steady feet, try your word and call a halt, "Wait! Wait a moment! We have not yet paid him for his service. Hold, till we can put this check in his hand!" The very mention of such a proposition flies back into your face as you see John Brown that victorious day.

Come with me to the market place in Rouen. See that remarkable figure they are bringing in their blundering blindness to the place of her world influence. She had done strange things. They piled the fagots around a bleak stake, and English soldiers, who tied her to her place, refused her request to have a crucifix, but one thrust up to her lips two sticks he snatched from the pyre and held them as a cross. "I can say my own mass," said she, as the poor priests refused her request; and that sounds to me like the first great announcements of a coming Protestantism. As the red flames and the choking smoke go curling up about the clean body and the cleaner spirit of the Maid of Orleans, try again your offer, "Here! Here! The world would like to pay this martyr. Someone give her this money." The very thought flies back in your face again in hotter fire than burned out that life that day.

Come with me again to that great square in Florence, the Piazza della Signoria. Was ever a stranger day in strange Italy? The preacher, before whose words the whole great city had been swayed, as reeds are swayed by strong winds, stood transfixed there where the soldiers brought him out to be burned. Come quickly, man, for the flames are leaping, and the crackling fagots make it hard for you to be heard. "Wait, wait," you shout, "Savonarola has not been settled with by the treasurer. Here is your gold, sir." The very words die on your lips, and the gold falls with vulgar clank to the pavement, as you shut your lips before the unpayable scene.

Come with me that oft delayed day, which finally came to that greatest human figure Christianity has yet constructed. They bring from stagnant, old Mamertine, that prison-bleached, bent-over, little old man, whose words had confounded kings, and put to flight all his accusers, and whose eloquent passion had won to his faith the soldiers chained to him, and the jailors who kept the gates. He kneels to bend his wonderful head across the block before the waiting axman. Just before he does so, he repeats a word just written, "I have fought a good fight. I have

finished my course. I have kept the faith."
Now's your chance. Speak quickly now. You
choke back the real words that are clamoring
within you, and try to speak, and you simply
turn away without a coarse word of pay being
framed at your lips.

Shall we dare go further in this pursuit?
Stagger as far as you can, on into the strangest
day that ever dawned across this strange world.
The Saviour of the world comes yonder down
that crooked little Jerusalem street, lifting and
dragging at a heavy cross, until he falls as they
turn around a corner. He comes on again, with
another to relieve him of the cross. Follow them
through that north gate and up that green hill.
Crowds are sitting there to watch him. I must
not drive words any further into such a scene. I
cannot pursue the idea I have been trying
through these familiar scenes to force to its own
refutation. I dare not say the word, coarse and
grating upon our finer appreciation, that we have
kept all through this sermon. God forgive me
if I have been guilty of even allowing my thought
to bring me too far now. We know when we
stand before Calvary that sacrifice must be its
own reward.

The really great things that have been done
upon this earth have been done as sacrifice.
There is no gold to pay. Whenever we really

arise to act like men and women at our best we
cannot be paid. Sacrifice is its own rule. It
must be its own reward. Only in this light can
we come to see the love of God. John has made
bold to lay the conclusions of all this squarely
before all his followers. The answer may be
found in anyone, who, under the higher sense of
sacrifice, will bring life and lay it clean on the
high altar of world service. By what plea can
any of us fail this call? I know it means sacrifice. I know there will be no pay set for induce-
ment. But the real meaning of this once appre-
ciated by any life, there can never again be for
that life any ease, other than that which is found
in the unfaltering performance of duty. "Only
he who bears himself well and faithfully in it all,
as part of it all, as debtor to it all, may hope to
be peacefully and forever above it all, by and by."

III

"A RENDEZVOUS WITH LIFE"

"I am crucified with Christ, nevertheless I live; yet not I, but Christ liveth in me: and the life which I now live in the flesh I live by the faith of the Son of God, who loved me and gave himself for me."—Gal. 2. 20.

WHEN a pendulum swings it always comes back. That is a trite sentence mechanically. It, however, is as true in the realm of thinking as it is in mechanics, and has been but little noticed there, though I will confess in my own little realm I have been practicing it to advantage for a long time. I have frequently set my attention to catch the reverse idea of some genuine thought. Not infrequently has the process suggested more constructive thought for my own experience than could be mine by the mere leadership in thought of another. Intellectually and experimentally I have found more profit in what an idea has germinated in my own mind, than in the bare idea suggested to me. Not that my thought was better than another, but that it is always more constructive to do one's own thinking than to humbly agree to what another has thought. The return swing of a good idea is always worth attention. I never fail to count on the return of a pendulum, but it is only by

constant effort I can bring my mind to turn
exactly in the opposite direction from a fine suggestion, and watch for the return swing. I
failed in this completely in the case disclosed
by the fine quoted theme of this sermon, a phrase
which carries all the more impressive meaning
because in reverse of one of the most famous
phrases that found a blood-red setting in the
war, and was not balanced in its meaning till
long after the war had laid down its mad
slaughter.

When the Great War was at its bloody worst,
and death was riding iron-hoofed over the strong
manly hearts of the world's strongest youth, and
young men's names were being scrawled all
across a mad world's news in dying; here and
there among the host of splendid fellows some
strong voice would speak impressively. Donald
Hankey arose with words well chosen and
couched in a heroism and fine fortitude that can
never, never cease to echo among us. Death
hushed his words suddenly. Robert Service
found a rare rhythm to which he set phrase to
heroism's highest call. Joyce Kilmer struck a
high note. Rupert Brooke sounded a strange,
clear tocsin. Charles Sorley, dead at twenty,
wrote:

> "Earth that never doubts nor fears,
> Earth that knows of death, not tears,

Earth that bore with joyful ease,
Hemlock for Socrates,
Earth that blossomed and was glad,
'Neath the Cross that Christ had;
Shall rejoice and blossom too,
When the bullet reaches you;
Wherefore, men marching
On the road to death sing,
Pour your gladness on earth's head,
So be merry, so be dead."

The dominant note of oratory and song and poem was death. Death was holding undisputed carnival all across the world. Death! Death! Death! We thought in terms of the dead. We schooled ourselves not to be afraid of death. Some folks even bragged that they discarded mourning. We were determined to look death out of countenance.

Of all the defiant words we ever framed into a phrase like a sharp javelin to hurl at the very heart of death, I believe it is everywhere agreed —I am sure it has never been questioned in my own impression—that the words of Alan Seeger took prime place. Big, strong, brave, clean, loyal, outstanding, cultured youth, threw that wonderful taunt at death:

"I have a rendezvous with Death,
At some disputed barricade,
When Spring comes back with rustling shade,
And apple blossoms fill the air;
I have a rendezvous with Death,
When Spring comes back, blue days and fair.

It may be he shall take my hand,
And lead me into his dark land,
And close my eyes, and quench my breath;
It may be I shall pass him still.
I have a rendezvous with Death,
On some scarred slope of battered hill,
When Spring comes round again this year,
And the first meadow-flowers appear.
God knows 'twere better to be deep
Pillowed in silk and scented down,
Where love throbs out in blissful sleep,
Pulse nigh to pulse, and breath to breath,
Where hushed awakenings are dear,
But, I've a rendezvous with Death,
At midnight in some flaming town,
When Spring trips north again this year
And I to my pledged word am true,
I shall not fail that rendezvous."[1]

That was poetry for war. War was writing there about as high as war could reach. More noble words have not been written on its bleeding page. Alan Seeger laid down his pen when he had written thus and walked out and kept his rendezvous. Death had no terrors for him, nor for the men who marched with him. War cannot be won by men who fear death out where shells fly thickest; nor can it be won when women who wait at home shall lose heart, and break because determined death is pounding at their fondest heart's affections.

[1]From *Poems*, by Alan Seeger. Used by permission of Charles Scribner's Sons, New York.

Someone has said that it was the victorious death of a young man that recreated the mere death story of the Passover with the promise of the resurrection. Jesus Christ, who there tasted death for every man, went straight through all that ghastly dying on Calvary's Cross to the great life which he made certain for everyone who would put their faith in him, in order that he might show us how triumphant life is over death after all.

We needed, and we waited for a finer note and challenge than war's challenge of death. Those were days for dying. War days. These are peace days! Days indeed for living! Who would give us the word to meet the day? We did not fear nor flee the rendezvous with death. It remained for another young man to speak. This one but eighteen years of age, and wearing the mortal shroud of a black skin. A Negro boy graduating from the high school in New York city found the phrase. His name is Countee Cullen, and for his unusual poem he has been given honorary scholarships in both New York and Columbia Universities.

> "I have a rendezvous with Life,
>   In days I hope will come,
>   Ere youth has sped, and strength of mind
>   Ere voices sweet grow dumb:
>   I have a rendezvous with Life
>   When Spring's first heralds hum.

It may be I shall greet her soon,
  Shall riot at her behest;
It may be I shall seek in vain
  The peace of her downy breast,
Yet I would keep this rendezvous,
  And deem all hardships sweet,
If at the end of the long white way,
  There life and I shall meet.

Sure some will cry it better far
  To crown their days in sleep,
Than face the wind, the road, the rain,
  To heed the calling deep.
Though wet, nor blow nor space I fear,
  Yet fear I deeply too,
Lest Death shall greet and claim me ere,
  I keep life's rendezvous."[1]

He has caught the same heroic and noble stride for peace, that seemed to conscript all our strength and sacrifice for war. And that has always been what peace has needed. Who can give us the call of heroics, and set our blood tingling with the conquest of peace? In war we sang bravely and marched unfalteringly out to meet death. In peace we must march no less heroically nor appealingly out to meet life. We must campaign with life. We must endure with life. We must triumph with life. The only thing that can choke fear at our throats will be, if we are going as we must go to go right, the fear,

   "Lest Death shall greet and claim us ere,
    We keep life's rendezvous."

---

[1] Used by permission of the author.

That is the gripping tragedy that forever lurks in the death of youth. Not that we fear to die, but that death at such a time shall have made us fail the privilege life really offered us. That was the great gaunt fact that swept with such horrible harvest in the tramp of war. We were wading along the bleeding way that materialism had dictated. It always leads to death. You cannot leave God out. We had dared try to do so. Society is not based on science, as some had been so sure it was; but, rather, as Dr. Burroughs has put it in fine compelling phrase, "not on science, but on con-science (conscience)." The sense and fear of God over all. Materialism grew death. War with its red, was the gigantic danger-signal to warn a whole misled world of its colossal mistake. Surely, none of us who are left to live on into to-day, so close out of the dying days of yesterday, will need any stronger argument for setting out to help build a new world on a better tradition. The tradition of God before all. The tradition of life. The conscription of life.

We arise, therefore, before the great youth of to-day to serve the conscription of a new and a demanding hour. We have conscripted them to death in that strange yesterday scarce gone. The little khaki tents standing on the street corners, and at the gates of public parks, we remember all so well. We conscripted them to death.

They marched away in those long, strange lines down which we looked through unintentional tears, and to which we shouted an offered courage. The last we heard of them so very, very often was the gripping long tones the bugler blew beside a low grave in the dark. Taps! Taps! Lights were out. All was over. They had not failed to keep their rendezvous with death.

Now we stand in peace, and conscript for life. There is a new roll from the drums. The long, long roll is hushed. Taps we do not call for now. The drums are beating a march. The ranks are formed. The bugle has sounded the reveille, and the buoyant sense of going to life is in the whole world to-day. We are calling everywhere that the same loyalty that found enthusiasm to death in war, shall now once more know it is called, and shall appreciate that not all the honor, and daring, and heroism of the world is set aside for the battlefield. "Peace hath her victories no less renowned than war." The courage that knew no falter before death is now to be paralleled by the courage that will not shrink before life.

I am sure there is none who would place any fairer honor than would I upon the graves of those brave men who went out, willing to die, and who did die for the victorious day which we of this unusual hour have inherited. I believe I know somewhat of the meaning of dying out there for the sake of a cause. I honor them for it. I stood beside them marching. I sat beside them dying. It took extreme courage. It took sheer nerve to hold their breasts against the biting steel in the night. It took all the bravery the heart could muster to stand at a muddy post all a dark night and unflinchingly wait the bitter steel that should strike death in. I honor them. I am grateful now for them. But, great and brave and noble that it all was, I am bound to say in justice to what they did, that it is more difficult for those of us who are left yet, to live into such a dearly bought day as is this, and to vindicate our right to inherit such a blood-bought heritage, than it was for those men to go out and die to bring it in. Who, oh, who am I, to dare reach out my poor little hand to receive from the red hands of suffering sacrifice the privilege of living in such a broad-gated day as is this? To take this preserved democracy of ours! To take this defended liberty of ours! To take this religious freedom of ours! Who, oh who am I to dare assume the right? Surely, I have now a rendezvous with life. It is harder to meet than the rendezvous with death. There is such constant strain. When death comes, I can steel myself and take the blow. I can bare my breast to the flash of his steel and dare him to do his worst. With the crash it is over and I have kept my rendezvous. But when I look life in the face, and set myself to keep tryst with life, I must know the strain of sustained endeavor. I must appreciate the continued fight of tireless monotony. I must gather strength for determined temptation. I must steel my soul for unkindness, and the falsehood of my hopes. I must preserve a determination not to surrender because I may stumble, and not to fall because I may have been tripped. Even if I do fall, I must struggle back to my feet while life yet throbs in my veins, and come on, come on, come on with life. If I actually do keep my rendezvous with life, I must know it is an indeterminate tryst I must maintain.

> "Sure some will cry it better far,
>   To crown their days in sleep,
> Than face the wind, the road, the rain,
>   To heed the calling deep.
> Though wet, nor blow nor space I fear,
>   Yet fear I deeply too,
> Lest Death shall greet and claim me ere
>   I keep Life's rendezvous."

It has now just been my repetitious privilege to go from school to school, to say a word to and witness the credentialed commissions of our prepared youth, as they start out into a practical world to test their ideals. War drained our colleges. It marched out the marshaled ranks till our halls of learning wore strange lonesomeness. But now once more peace has crowded our colleges. With the tocsins of war hushed awhile (which, may God grant, shall yet be stretched into forever), I wish we might write life in as heroic terms as war sought to write death. Why should war and death carry the brilliant banners, and wear the most glittering uniforms, and march to the most inspiring music? Why should war, leading to rampant death, fly in our faces everything to dazzle, and drive prancing horses, and be lifted with sweeping huzzahs, while peace shall be handed a pale banner and made to fly the symbol of a dove, and be robbed of a bugle, while it shall be lulled into the soft ways of quiet to the soothing tones of a lute? I am for heroism in life. I would point our noblest youth to the victories of peace. To the great genuine darings to which life leads. To the supremely fine comradeships which life offers. To the brave adventures life discloses. To the noble services life makes vivid. Life not death is our calling. A rendezvous with life.

> "My only fear is,
> Lest Death shall greet and claim me ere
> I keep Life's rendezvous."

I do not want death to break my rendezvous with life.

"Carry on! Carry on!
Fight the good fight and true;
Believe in your mission, greet life with a cheer;
There's big work to do, and that's why you are here,
Carry on! Carry on!
Let the world be the better for you,
And at last when you die, let this be your cry,
Carry on, my soul, carry on."

That, after all, is the reward of it all. There is nothing a man will give in exchange for his life, but there are things which a man will give his life in exchange for, and never again recall the bargain. All that is, in the fine consolation which always goes with the sacrifice attendant upon the response of your life. The genuine compensation for the life of real service in this world has ever been the same. Whenever life is actual ministry it is a joy. There may have been the hidden method of a paradox in the way Jesus said it, but he was telling us in brilliant phraseology the very finest truth in which we can write life, when he said, "He that willeth to save his life shall lose it; but he that loseth his life for my sake, the same shall find it." Jesus knew more about human nature than all others ever will know. Self-giving somehow leads mysteriously back to life. "The most living man," said Paul Sabatier, "is he who gives, forgets, sacrifices himself."

These are days for the living. We are called

to live, and to live this day of ours so living may be called real life, and may not be misrepresented by smalling ideals. We are on the life side of the great sacrifice. Whether we personally be willing or unwilling that any should go and die for us, they have already died for us. Unworthy though we be, we have a life to live this side that dying.

Job has phrased a wonderful question in one of his most significant utterances. "Hast thou commanded the morning . . . and caused the dayspring to know his place?" Commanding the morning? Taking possession of the day to be. Morning is the time to mold the whole day with your specific intentions. Youth is life's morning. Have you commanded the morning? Life is in my plea now. The running of the years is heard across this hour. If strong men made tryst with death, and marched bravely to it in war, surely strong men, and women too, will make tryst now with life, and march bravely to it in peace. To me to live is Christ. I will keep Life's rendezvous.

IV

COAT AND CLOAK

"If any man will sue thee at the law, and take away thy
coat, let him have thy cloak also."—Matt. 5. 40.

SUCH words as these, even from the lips of
Jesus, sound strange, and in the interpretation
of ordinary conduct, seem to be beyond all rea-
sonable practice. They were emphasized to me
recently by a man, a business man, a man to
whom all rules of conduct are flavored by business methods. He came to me in the spirit of
complaint, a condition born perhaps in the fact
that his practice and his convictions were not
perfectly synchronized. He said he was both-
ered over a plain-spoken passage of Scripture.
What it says is easy to read, but what it means
is hard to believe. It is that passage, said he,
which exhorts me to a liability after a suit in
court, and declares that if a man shall take my
coat by law, I am also to hand him my cloak. I
felt as I listened to his manner of quotation, and
witnessed the comment he made, with his teeth
tight set in the determination of resistance, that
he had just been to court, and had lost some
clothes. He said, "The man who sues me gets

only what the law allows." How ordinary that sounds! That is the sure reception of great fundamentals of conduct by ordinary ideals of practice.

The complaint of the man, however, fastened my attention to this verse, and revealed to me one of the most helpful rebukes to every smalling idea of my conduct I have ever found, in the always wonderful words of Jesus Christ.

One of the most outstanding distinguishments of the things Jesus said is to be found in the manner in which he lifted into universal interpretation the ordinary actions of ordinary folks. It is a heartening thing to me in my own little life, if I can be made to feel that the things I do, run away from their mere doing into an expression in meaning, to all life everywhere. Jesus was forever doing that very thing to the people with whom he talked. With divine fingers he would touch with radiant interpretation some little action, and thus stand it up in an immortality of meaning. A poor woman, in embarrassed approach one day, broke a tiny box of perfumery as the offering of her appreciation, and our Lord set that incident to make sweet all the ages to come. A widow came timidly down the corridors of the great Temple in the conscious poverty of her little offering, to quietly drop the least gift that could be left in the great collection-box where gold and silver rang the confident offerings of the rich. But she was seen of Jesus, and her gift that day has been the inspiration for the givers of the world ever since. A cup of cold water given in his name has become a new symbol of service. I need not mention more of the many. I only seek thus to say that Jesus saw the heart of every action, and with divine touch exposed it to its lasting meaning.

He saw the court in action. Men were mad there. Men were in sharp contest there for their rights. Everything that is taken from any hand by law must be pulled from unwilling fingers. Men are not convinced at law; they are compelled. They go to law to get justice, but the man from whom so-called justice is extracted never appreciates as justice anything which is taken from him. What they get from me at court they will be compelled to pry loose! Thus I approach the law. I go there either to hold tight my last right, or I go to compel the last ounce of flesh due me.

Jesus saw all that, and in trying to define the way a Christian life should be lived he said, When you go to court, and a man sues you, and takes away your coat, get right up, strip it off, and hand it over to him. Then you and the law are straight. But you are a Christian. When the law is met then Christianity has its chance.

Other folks will do just as you do when compelled to give up your coat. Everyone is alike at law. Take my coat. But when you begin making life yourself, and begin to deal in things you can help, and set yourself to do things you choose to do, there Christianity becomes visible in action.

So, when the law-empowered man reaches out his law-exhorted hand and takes your coat, don't let him get away with only that. If you do, it will be merely a case at law, and there are so many, many law cases. What you are to do is to exceed the verdict. Hold on, my brother! Come here. Don't hurry out with your coat. Take this cloak too. It was meant to go with the coat, and they look good together. Allow me to throw this over your shoulders. That is a new idea in court. Justice has been outstepped. Justice is matter of law. Christianity must forever step out beyond the statutes. What influence could you have if you were always willing to stop at the hard edge of compulsion? The man who works in the chain-gang on our streets, and is led about by an armed guard and shown just what he is to do; that poor gun-driven wretch is a fair picture of the service of compulsion. He does what he has to do. Take my coat, will you? Here it is! You have it, but that is absolutely all you are going to get from me. Oh, don't stop there, my friend, or you will be dumped out in the great mass of court decisions and be lost.

There must be an excess in religion. It is that cloak after the coat which creates that peculiar atmosphere in which alone the Christian character can mature. No man at his best is ever satisfied in doing only what he is compelled to do. We must exceed the rule. We must outrun the law. We must go beyond justice. There was told not long before he died a fine little story about the "Laird of Skibo," Andrew Carnegie. In the lovely grounds about his great Scotch home he had a wonderful rose garden. It was a perfect riot of bloom, and a dense fragrance. The villagers were allowed free access to the garden, and there were no signs. The paths among the flowers were thronged by the glad people, who were constantly helping themselves to the tempting blooms that nodded in unforbidden reach. One day the head gardener came to the great rich man and brought a bitter complaint. He had worked hard to grow the flowers. His judgment was that the garden did not reflect the work he had done because the unrestrained people kept the flowers picked off. He said to the master: "I wish to inform you, sir, that the village folk are plucking the roses in your garden. They are denuding your rose-trees, sir."

"Ah," said Mr. Carnegie, gently, "I understand you I believe. My neighbors are fond of the flowers are they? They keep the bushes plucked do they? Then you will have to plant more roses."

Well, all that is merely a modern revised version of what Jesus was saying here; it is said in terms of flowers instead of clothes. You think you lost your suit at the jury box when the man got your coat. If you did, you had better make sure to win it in your own jurisdiction when you can go along with him and bestow your cloak. He can win your coat. You can give him your cloak. The coat is his. The cloak is yours.

This excess of our religion is, after all, the characteristic distinction we are to have. We are not merely to keep the law. Everybody is supposed to do that. The Christian must always be far ahead of keeping the law. "What do ye more than others?" is a Bible inquiry that is legitimate in asking of us always. It may be a sufficient record for mere morality to be able to say at least that it was never in jail. But the excess of life which lies out beyond the keeping of the law is the qualification which makes life really Christian. To be what we must be, and to do what we must do is narrow and uninteresting. I am suspicious of, and afraid to trust

the man who forever carries the code under his
arm, and hunts for the last legal decision. He is
out for keeping the law, and he will not keep
in his possession any more than he is compelled
to keep.

There is to me a tinge of injustice in the man
who is always asking for justice. It sounds so
limited. It seems so rigidly measured. A man
can be just, and only just, and just just is not
very just. Shakespeare has portrayed it all so
wonderfully in old Shylock, who, always crying
for justice, had at last to suffer the contentment
that was offered in sheer justice. The judge
never seemed more just than when the law was
read and the pound of flesh was required. That
old, bitter, eager, mean pleader for justice took
the scale and the scalpel, and began to dig away
the clothes from the left breast of his debtor that
he might there cut out his just reward. Just a
moment: The trembling justice hunter paused.
A pound of flesh it says here. Yes sir, a pound.
See then that there be not one grain more than
a pound or less than a pound cut from that
breast. You want justice, now take it. See thou
also that no drop of blood be taken or shed. This
calls for flesh and not blood. No blood is
required, neither will any blood be tolerated.
There stood that law-clad man obtaining justice
only to find that justice may be turned into a

sentence rather than an award upon the crier for justice only.

You cannot be arrested as long as you keep the law, exactly, but life consists of so much more than merely not being arrested. The constant injunction for Christian character in conduct is that it shall add excess to justice and thus make them both beautiful. The cloak I can give is far more expressive of my life than the coat you can take from me at court. I would dread to go out of this world at last and leave a record that no one ever got anything from me, but what the law allowed them. They got my coat, but that was all. That is writing life in its littling decisions. Christianity deals in greater things. Here is my cloak. Take it, and welcome. That is where I get real expression. That cloak stands for all those finer expressions we cherish in each other. All our littleness and meanness and unworthiness can keep their places in our hearts while we accept the findings of the court. But just as soon as the verdict is rendered, and our coats are taken away, then in the realm where we proffer our cloak too, all those little things begin to fall behind. The great rule of Christian conduct has stamped out the idea that for any man merely what he has to be is enough. The real noble things in my life are those which no statute can demand and no court can award. Sue me if you will. All you can get is my coat. My cloak you will never get unless I choose to come along after the trial and offer it. Jesus was telling us in this keen verse that life by compulsion is little life.

God himself acts thus. He made the world that way. Excess lies everywhere. If a flower had to be made to propagate a plant, it could have been made on a plain pattern and in dull colors and free from fragrance. Why scallop those strange patterns of orchids? Why paint poppies with such flaming faces? Why laden heliotrope with such fascinating perfume? I will tell you exactly why. This is God's world, and he couldn't make a cheap world and keep his own personality. This universe was not let out by contract to the cheapest bidder. God did not need to make a diamond. The fields would be just as rich to feed us. The rocks would be just as strong to shelter us. God did not need to make a ruby. But this is God's world, and you could not expect him to make a mere utilitarian world. He is forever beyond compulsion. He wants his people to find the same great truth for themselves.

We are living in a growingly regulated day. More and more conduct is being mechanically prescribed. We hear the click of the meter. The self-computing scale is read on both sides to pro-

tect the butcher and convince the purchaser.
We buy everything with mechanics. The meter
is set to everything we use. You hear it when
you turn on your faucet to get a drink, when
you open your book to read, when you talk on
your phone. We are metered. What an outstanding chance in such a day for real abounding life! The finest thing anyone can do with
the abundance of life is to bestow it. That was
the distinguishing contrast in Jesus' great life
to those people then, and it remains so to us now.
He was ever going beyond compulsion, and you
cannot watch his ways and fail to appreciate
that a measure of necessity is no just way to
measure a real life. What eloquent sincerity
forever attended him! He walked so divinely in
his human conduct that blind foolish men crucified him one mad, dark day. Yonder beneath his
cross, squatting in a selfish circle of carelessness,
the soldiers attendant actually could be seen
throwing dice for the possession of his coat.
Who will get his coat? And they gambled on,
and darkness was creeping over the foolish multitude who watched. But when he died there; died
because he gave himself a ransom, that was
something new, and those gambling soldiers
who could take his coat, seeing that he alone
could give his life, cried out in conviction,
"Surely, surely this must have been the Son of

God." From that day, all those with whom this Lord and Master has walked have felt their hearts burn within them by the way.

Whoever expected me to carry any less than the abounding measure of conduct in my Christian activities! I cannot be small there. I cannot stop at the court. What the tax levy can pull from me will leave me no distinction. The law can take any coat. Go on then; your cloak is your opportunity. Whenever God gets into your life you may be sure to be pushed on, and men will know you by the unfailing sign. Have I now the attention of one who has been, or is now, troubled with the conviction that thus far life has been too limited? Have you sat down in a dogged resistance to say, that all they ever got from you they had to sue you for, and when they did get your coat you were sure it wasn't much of a coat anyhow. That is the meanest, littlest sort of a conviction you ever tried to live with. Every one of us in our better moments feels ashamed that we have not been able to bless others more than we have. We look over the town, and the whole wide world in its great calling need, and against it all there is our little coat. That is all we have done. And we did that by compulsion. They sued us for it. It never was much of a coat either. But when we see it there, as absolutely all there is to represent us in the big demanding work life really presents, we do not care to claim it. Someone steps up to us, and, looking out over what has been done in a needy day, inquires, "What did you give?" And we make answer without daring to look up, or pointing out any particular coat, "Oh, just one of those coats in the big pile there." And the answer is a confession of shame and dissatisfaction. I wish I could do more. Here, take my cloak! And our great Leader and Saviour, and Redeemer, and Example says, "That sounds Christian." You cannot walk with Jesus Christ the shortest way, and fail to hear the call for your cloak. Your required coat will not satisfy your life. As a Christian you are compelled to acknowledge that a man may begin for himself, but he can never end there.

This is the drum-beat of life's real march. It is the Christian compulsion of overpowering indebtedness. We are not to simply discharge our obligations to our fellow beings. We are bound by a more sacred debt. A contribution is asked of us to the invisible interests of the universe. We are here not to be sued for our debts. We are here privileged to bestow our gifts. In God's name we are among men. We may be required our coats. We can give our cloaks.

V

GOD'S MAN

"I sought for a man among them, that should make up the hedge, and stand in the gap before me for the land."
—Ezek. 22. 30.

God's man! A somewhat presumptuous theme to announce. I would not, however, interpret it so, but, rather, would I seek with you to take my stand where I can hear plainly what God wants with me. Find me someone who can fill up the gap in the hedge, and stand before me for the land! The call thrills me. I wish I might be thus used. Is there not some place where I can stand effectually? Cannot this request be interpreted in some way that will put conscription to every power I have in the task of my Lord? I do want to fit in with God's great purpose on this earth. I have long ago driven from my soul the small desire to find something that will bring easy pleasure to me. I honestly long to be useful. Here am I, Lord; send me!

I believe fundamentally lodged in all our hearts there may be found a genuine desire to really be of service to God. It sounds, of course,

presumptuous to say God needs any man. There
is a great and a very true sense in which he
does not need any man. Don't you ever dare
get proud, and spread yourself like a green bay
tree, or any other sort of a shrub. Don't lift
your confident head. God can get on. He man-
aged somehow before you arrived. The organi-
zation of his purpose will continue even after
you are gone. You are not necessary. But there
is another sense, and a very true one too, and
inspiring, in which God needs everyone, even me;
poor, weak, ignorant, blundering me. He has
a place for me. It has been inspiringly true that
God has diligently searched through every age
and generation, for the very one he was in particular need of. God's man! The one who
would make up the hedge, and actually stand in
the gap. When he has been found, and the hedge
has been completed, and the gap closed, then
and there has been discovered a character
upon whom the ages concentrated. There is an
old story, I have heard it ever since I was a boy.
Preachers have told it, teachers have used it for
pupils, parents have told it to their children. I
presume the best credential it carries is that we
have all heard it so often it is familiar. One day
in a trying moment of a great battle the Duke
of Wellington called a gallant young officer to
take his company and capture a very destructive

battery of the enemy that was pouring its deadly
fire upon his men from the crest of a strategic
hill. Everyone knew the price of the duty to
which the officer and his men were assigned.
The gallant young soldier turning to the great
leader said, "I can go, sir, if you will but give me
one clasp of your all-conquering hand." The
clasp was granted, and the brave man went
straight to his duty under the streaming eyes of
interest of him whose orders he was keeping.

God always needs a man. The crisis is forever
on. A crisis is a matter of so universal application that it is adjusted in crucial circles where
we all find strategic place. To every one of us
life has an adjustment that makes us essential.
Some hedge has a gap where we are needed.
Nor must we allow that crying gap that day to
monopolize the idea of importance. If all the
rest of the essential hedge had not been in place,
the crisis would not have been a mere story of
one gap. The faithfulness of the whole hedge
stands testified to in the fact that but one place
is lacking. It would have been easy to develop
just as great a cry of need on every hand, had
not kindred faithfulness been everywhere to that
which was called for merely to complete what
was almost done. Only one man was needed.
That was testimony conclusive to a goodly faithfulness already provided. I thank God every

day of my life for the faithful. We are liable to forget them in the directed attention which falls to the place revealed because some one did fall out. After all, the glory of the whole safety is not to be seen in the one who upon heroic call comes faith to meet a crisis, but must, rather, be recognized in the great number of the faithful who kept the defense so complete that but one place was lacking.

Life is so adjusted that every one of us must be compelled to accept judgment before the place we ourselves alone can fill. The judgment of every individual must forever stand upon his or her own impossible-to-be-delegated duty. To some the circle of the hedge is larger; to some it is smaller. But life is to every human soul answerable at a crisis. Yours may be discovered in the hedge of a family; yours in the hedge of a neighborhood, or of a city, or of a state, or of a nation. Sometimes men have been drawn in large enough measure to be compelled to meet their judgment before the crisis of the world.

One day a cry, quite similar to this we have taken from Ezekiel, was heard from Jeremiah. It was a day of great need, and the prophet called out, "Run ye to and fro through the streets of Jerusalem, and see . . . if ye can find a man." There were doubtless men in Jerusalem then, as there were in the days of Ezekiel—good

men, and clean men too. King Josiah and
Baruch and Zephaniah, could have been easily
enlisted. They were helpful men. Many other
noble men were doubtless to be had there. But
they were in seclusion. Evil was rampant in the
streets. Goodness was under cover. A defiant
champion of righteousness was needed.

How would you know when you had found a
man? By what test would you make sure of
your discovery before you made bold to answer
the cry of the prophet, and say, "Here is a man"?
What standard of conduct will you use? How
do you know it will be acceptable? I was drawn
to read the other day a bold poster headed with
attractive letters, "The Ideal Man." But it was
a disappointment, for it was the measured
exactness of the body a tailor wanted to dress.
He should weigh a certain number of pounds,
and stand at a certain height, and wear a collar
of a prescribed size, and with hat and shoes
that met the test, he was the tailor's ideal. But
they had a large collection of just such measurements at the penitentiary where I had recently
spoken, and over whose great registration charts
I had been looking. Ideal bodies were there.
Bodies that had to some been among the prime
causes of their downfall. A young man with a
devout faith in a peculiar superstition asked me
one day how tall I was. I told him I was just

six feet tall. He immediately said I was mistaken. I told him I knew how tall I was, and was prepared to meet his dispute, when he said with that strange confidence which seems to abide undisturbed in folks when they become obsessed with some freak notion: "No, you are not just six feet tall. There never has been but one who was exactly six feet in height. Jesus Christ alone stood there, and none shall ever again attain the exact stature." I left that young man with his strange superstition that there was somehow a divinity in six feet of mortality. I looked carefully over the complex tabulation of men called criminals, as recorded by that very sure system of identification called the Bertillon measurements. There was but one chance in thirteen million of the identification ever failing. Long decimal fractions, minutely describing all the unchanging bony parts of a body. But there was no agreement. Every measure was to be found there. There is no criminal stature. Even as there is no divinity in six feet, there is likewise no criminality in five feet six inches. There is no set stature for a man. You cannot find him with a yard stick. I know where there lives a man who boasts of no ideal measure in his physical equipment. He is a misfit at every shop. His body is wracked and broken. But in manhood he is richly endowed. Some years ago one of the most confident self-styled prophets of human estimate was a man named Lavater. He called himself a physiognomist. He studied the shapes of men's heads, the angle of their brows, and the bulge in the skull just above their ears. He was handed two photographs, and informed that one of the men whose picture he held was a notorious highwayman who had been hung for his crimes, and was asked to pick the picture and explain the reason. He was not slow to make his selection, and offer his analysis. There can be no mistake on this, said he, as he held one picture up. Note the penetration of the eye, and the capacious brow. All that shows meditation. Here is easily the picture of a man who reasons deeply. Here is analysis and synthesis. This man is a great mentality. Then holding the other picture up he declared that the utter lack of all these things he had been listing from one face were the sure testimony of the villain. When he had finished, he was surprised to learn, that he had actually selected Immanuel Kant, the great philosopher and founder of critical philosophy, author of *Critique of Pure Reason,* as a highway robber, and had ascribed to the robber the place of the philosopher. Who will provide us standards of judgment in our search for a man?

There are always crises in life. Hedges are incomplete. Gaps are begging for attention. God's effort with Israel, leading them forward to a place where they could be of temporary service to the great ultimate world issue, is one continuous narration of the solicitation of the Most High for someone who would be bold enough to make up the hedge in a crisis. The men who have the prominent places in this great Book of God, are those whose lives in some way were able to be fitted into the gap. There stands Moses against the wickedness and idolatry of the people. He struck the golden calf from their altar and destroyed it before their rebuked gaze, as he made up again the broken hedge of religious faithfulness. There stands Josiah. He heard the call, and came forward to take his place and purge Judah and all the land from the high places and groves and images and false altars, they had allowed built among them. There stands Nehemiah. The people had broken down the hedges of their faithfulness by doing unlawful things on the Lord's Day. The rugged prophet threw himself into the gap and made up the defense of the land again. The whole history of God's work for his people has been so. O God, give us men! Great men! Good men! Brave men! True men! Suncrowned men! There are so many broken places. Sin has uprooted so much of the best defense of the race. It has broken down the walls. Made great breaches in churches, in cities, in estates, in families, in friendships. Before all these sadly broken places to-day we cannot but feel the impelling call of the need of our best heroisms. It follows the call of our text, however, to say quite impressively, that God was displeased, for he looked that someone would show a public spirit and oppose the sinful practices. But no one responded. Oh for God's necessary man. Sodom could have been saved had it but been able to find the men. But its hedge was broken down. You cannot read down the eloquent story of history and fail to hear this call on almost every page. The day the city of Nola fell captive to the great Roman armies, the Roman censor ordered at once the good men of the town to be brought before him. The old City Host who was ordered to bring the hostages, made his sorrowful way out to the sacred cemetery, and there in the painful admission of the city's living poverty, called and called at the graves of the dead, for he knew not where to call for a good man among the living. We do not admit the calamity of Nola, but do feel that the condemnation of our day is because of the fact that so many of our strong men are not in determined sacrifice standing in the gapping places of best service.

I would make two direct statements, one an appeal and one a declaration. I would first emphasize the outstanding need that strong folks shall appreciate the call of God. One day I was walking across the city of Rome, in company with a very interesting student of archæology, listening to his constant comment on matters of historic interest, which were on every side. He said as we walked beside their famous river: "Note that bit of a ruined buttress there at the river's edge. That is the site of the bridge of Horatius." How the name leaped to my soul in heroics.

> "In yon straight path, a thousand,
>   May well be stopped by three,
>   Now who will stand on either hand,
>   And keep the bridge with me?"

So I cared not how poor might be the authority for the fastening of the good old story to that particular little pile of stones before me, it was the memory of the heroic story that made me glad.

> "How well Horatius kept the bridge,
>   In the good, brave days of old."

A strong man for the gap! What is strength for, if not to build out danger? The axiomatic conduct of every ability should be to find its most useful place and there to take its stand. In

reading along the route of that interesting
Frenchman Mirabeau, I came upon an incident
of one of his ancestors who was a colonel in the
army. Because of his rare bravery he had been
given charge of a bridge, the defense of which
was very important in the battle. From his
favored place the general of the day kept constant watch of every part of the field with special interest for the keeping of the bridge. With
ever rising admiration he witnessed column
after column of the enemy's ranks hurled
against that bridge-head only to fall back broken
in defeat. Finally upon a renewed and determined charge upon the crucial point, the general
watching the action through his glasses, saw as
the smoke lifted, the streaming ranks of the
enemy pouring across the bridge. He closed his
field glasses and made the conclusive comment
in a short sentence of confidence, "Mirabeau is
dead." As long as that dauntless man stood in
the gap there was no place for fear at his post.
The only liability there was to be found in his
death.

> "The kings of eternal evil,
>   Still darken the hills about;
> Thy part e'en with broken saber,
>   To rise on the last redoubt,
> To fear no sensible failure,
>   Nor court the game at all,
> But fighting, fighting, fighting;
>   Die! driven against the wall."

Never you mind dying. That may be God's chance to you. Stand to your place. Live if you may. Die if you must. Don't fail to be there. I cannot conceive of any more inspiring expectation for a man of strength than the fact that God has somewhere for him a serious place which he can fill, and thus help save the world. How anyone could ever lose interest in such a task, or grow wearied in such a task, or feel justified in quitting such a task, or allow anything to displace the call to such a task, I cannot see. Would that these poor and ill-chosen words of mine might utterly die out now in the voice of God, till every one of you, whose attention may be here set, would be compelled to interpret your endowment as the obligation of your lives. God needs you now. The church strangely halts in many because some of you have not been in your place. There are gaps in the church hedge. Places vacated where some of you once nobly stood. Hath not Satan crept in and wrought consternation? Crept in where your courage, or your tenderness, or your business ability, or your faithfulness might have served. There is a certain measure of failure somewhere to-day, that would have been fenced out, had you but made up the hedge and been faithful. It might be true that the condemnation you so easily seem able to fasten upon the church to-day is there

with attendant blame upon you who seem able to
detect the failure in the thing in which you are
strong. Whenever a man of keen business ability
is ready to expose the unbusinesslike methods in
the churches' conduct, I would urge him to
appreciate his peculiar obligation to help make
up the lack he seems so qualified to discern. The
same argument holds against every interpretation. There is a call of God to you in the break
in the hedge you so easily can see. Step into
the gap, sir! There is your place. God will
certainly hold you accountable for what you see
and yet refuse to fulfill.

The second observation I make now is that the
hope of the world is in the ability of Christianity
to make genuine men abound among us, and do
their duty. The responsibility that has been put
upon the church of Christ, sent out with divine
commission to save the world, is to raise up
faithful men, Christian men who will stand in
all the gaps, and make up the hedge, and stand
for God before the land.

The most irresistible appeal I know is the obligation of ability. I cannot see how it can be
avoided. It is what makes selfishness look so
little and mean. Who gave you your strength,
and what obligation lies in its possession? What
right has any human soul to sit to monopolize
its own ability, and lavish it upon its own selfish

desire? If but once we could get men to look
upon their ability as their obligation to God!
If they would but interpret their strength in
terms of ability to serve! If they would but
catch the drum-beat of expectation in the divine
call, "He that would save his life must lose it!"
These great lifting "ifs" are the haunt of every
preacher's message. When they have been
removed by heroic espousals, there invariably
has been wrought out the great life of service.
There go the heroes! Paul, shouting ever as he
sets himself into labors abundant, endeavoring
only to discharge the great indebtedness which
seemed to conscript every power he possessed.
He never tired at his task, ever conscious
though he was that his debt never would be paid
until he had bestowed all he could be upon a
world that needs every man's best laid upon its
high altar in sacrifice. Such has been the never-
varying story of heroics. Who follows in this
train?

What, sir, have you to answer before this need-
struck day through which you are living? What
have you done? What are you doing now to help
a most significant transitional era find its true
way, and keep up its courage, and get round to
the right? When I bring myself as a preacher to
look straight at such a call as that, it seems to
me that God cannot tolerate any of us in his

pulpits who cannot convince men unanimously to act upon it. What right have I to preach such a compelling gospel if I cannot find word and figure to make it imperative? If the gaps are but pointed out, how can it be possible that any shall sit careless and unconcerned if they possess the strength to fill them? There was a fine compelling admiration we all felt at the old story of the regiment from whose ranks but ten men were desired to go to a task so serious as to be almost certain death in enlistment. When volunteers were called for, every man in the regiment with one united tread stepped out and said, "Send me!" With this great day, and its great task challenging us, I cannot believe the opportunity presented by the Christian commission can fail of response. Have I not in this simple appeal now found the chord to which your souls vibrate? Does not the obligation of your ability to fill up some gap in the hedge find response in your highest sense of privilege? Because you can fill up that gap, you ought to do so. That broken defense before you is your personal condemnation.

I know full well what the temptation of power is. The story of human relationship has it all too plainly written across its every page. The temptation of power, whatever its form may assume, is always the same. It is to search out some strategic place where it can commandingly take its stand and charge the world toll. Pay me for my wisdom! Pay me for my genius! Pay me for my talent! Pay me! Pay me! I am strong enough to collect tribute from the world, and it should congratulate itself that I am here. The strong man is forever tempted to set himself up for tribute. Egotism is easy. It seems natural for all weakness to have to pay for its shortcoming.

But the vital message of our Christianity comes into collision with all such misinterpretation of power. The spirit of the life of Jesus, and of his wonderful and revolutionizing message, and of his perfectly consecrated life and death and life again, was and is, "For their sakes I sanctify myself." Under the spell of such leadership in devotion as our Christ has given us, we must conclude that a man has not begun to breathe the real sense of his power until he shall have become enamored of an overpowering moral indebtedness. Greatness has not taken root in our hearts until we recognize that within us is some power to help and better the world, and that power, whatever it may be, has made full and heroic response in service. No speech was ever made by Roman orator that carried more eloquence in conviction than that short speech of the brave man who rode forth at the challenge for the most precious gift the city could make, and as he gave himself even in the superstition of their blind error said as death reached for him, "Rome has no more precious gift than a Roman citizen." Devotion like that, thrilling as it is, when set to the fine ministry of Christianity, is compelling. Let the strong men and the strong women hear it! Let the cultured men and women hear it! This is a plea tuned to eternal heroics. Culture, knowledge, practical skill, taste, riches, any form of power is impaired and perverted to the degree in which it misses the element of ministry, holds itself absolved from debt to mankind, and regards man as its own debtor. "You are not your own!" "You are bought with a price!" "No man liveth to himself." Oh, if but once the great absorbing task of lifting this world to God, would fall as a passion upon our strong ones! If we could but awaken the active interest of the men and the women who have strength that seems commensurate, what a thrill would run along the ranks of world endeavor! Every gap in the hedge is a claim of God upon our assistance. There is the great gap of ignorance calling for the attention of the learning of the world. What is culture and education for but to build out ignorance and fill up the gap through which so much sorrow and suffering has poured in upon the race? You, with refinement and education, have no right to sit down to your little selfish place and keep the good ministry of such things to yourselves. This is God's call.

There are the big dangerous gaps of impurity, and stupidity, and degradation. I need not now call the long list of the danger places. Enough now to say the hedge is not made up and the gaps stand calling. God points to your duty. I know this is not easy, but we have not been called to ease here. I know this is not comfortable, but I have not learned in the way of my Lord that he was greatly concerned here now for the way where comfort may be found. This is indeed burdensome. But ahead of us there goes the One who not only called us to bear burdens, but went his great divine way with the sins of a whole world upon him. I know you do not need to respond to such a call. Quite within men's power has it always been to make mere epicures of themselves, and dawdle life away, and leave the world to stumble on. That is your preroga- tive. It goes with being a man. The gap in the hedge that you can fill, can also be refused by you, and you can go somewhere apart and spend yourself upon yourself. Aaron Burr did it. He was called of God once. He was moved of the Spirit. He was touched in a revival with gen- uine interest. He was a rare youth too. He had

the stuff of victory in him. His was the blood
of the best. But he refused. He deliberately
chose to turn his back on duty. He went his own
way. He left that open gap. That was Aaron
Burr. The prerogative of manhood has always
made possible the refusal of God's call. It has
always enabled men to shirk the gap, and take
what they have called their ease. Let the hedge
fall down! Let the gap gap! That is humanity's
prerogative. God cannot keep man as man and
command him against his will. But to-day as of
old, and always until the work shall be done,
God help us, he seeks for a man who will make
up the hedge and stand in the gap. Who, then,
this day will come forth in the name of the King?
Who this day is ready to offer his life to the
task? I cannot believe you will fail him. I
know you will not allow the enemy to break
through and come in upon our cause for the painful reason that you were not in your place. I
claim you therefore right now for this calling
task. "Only he who bears himself well and faithfully in it all, as part of it all, as debtor to it all,
may hope to be peacefully and forever above it
all by and by."

VI

MAN'S GOD

"Hast thou not known? Hast thou not heard that the everlasting God, the Lord, the Creator of the ends of the earth, fainteth not, neither is weary? There is no searching of his understanding. He giveth power to the faint; and to them that have no might he increaseth strength. Even the youths shall faint and be weary, and the young men shall utterly fall; but they that wait upon the Lord shall renew their strength; they shall mount up with wings as eagles; they shall run, and not be weary; and they shall walk, and not faint."—Isa. 40. 28-31.

ANY one of numerous passages of Scripture might here be taken for a text to express the fact of human expectation in God. The passage we choose here, to text this talk with, is not taken for any purpose of analysis, as disclosing the full description of the God of our race, but, rather, as a familiar, and universally accepted as a beautiful passage, that puts in living phrases some of the elements that refresh our souls in faith.

In the sermon preceding this we were considering "God's Man." Now I wish to reverse the words and face the meaning couched in the oppoite consideration, "Man's God." I was trying in the former sermon to drive to meaning in all our souls the searching fact that God has an

expectation in every one of us. It stiffens my
shoulders to know there is genuine expectation
in me. When my country shall make plain to
me that somewhere, somehow, I can be of service,
I straighten myself to accept the task, and
silence whatever fears may seek to arise and say,
"I will give my time, my talent, my possessions,
even my life, that my country shall not be disappointed in me." When my home and my
family take refuge behind me, and let me see
myself as one in whom they place faith, and on
whom they depend, then I stiffen my purpose
toward a world, where a living is sometimes hard
to dig out, and set my heart to a life of virtue
and honor, amid whatever temptations may rise,
and declare I will not disappoint that expectation in me. When my God lays his hand upon
poor unknown me, and says to me that I am
needed by him in the task of holding this world
toward righteousness, and that I can make up
the hedge, and fill up some gap, and stand before
him for the land, then I feel a strange thrill running through my soul which greatens my measure
in divine expectation. I am ready to set myself
into whatever life may throw at me and declare
that if my stand in my place can be of positive
service to my God, I will stand there, I will
endure there, I will be true there, I will die
there; I simply will not fail God. There is a

strengthening in life which comes to me when I am assured that I am trusted.

All that, however, is the smallest side of our religion. The least of my religion to me is what I can do, even at my best. I fear me we are endangered these days of overemphasizing the human side of our religion. After all the best I can do is pitifully little; I am ashamed of it. The strongest I can possibly be is pitifully weak; I am ashamed of it. If I shall dare frame my sense of religion around myself, it will stand to a small and frail measure indeed. The encouragement and inspiration of my religion to me is not to be found in me, but, rather, in God with me. I stumble dreadfully. I stagger even in my best endeavors. I fail even when I lift my highest purposes. But that is not my religion. My religion looks the other way. My hope is in God. My strength is in God. When I stumble to fall, I find then the everlasting arms are under me. When I lose my way in the gloom which gathers to pitch darkness about me so often, I always find the readiness of my help long promised to guide me with his all-seeing eye. When I am discouraged, and broken, and forsaken, and alone, then even though my father and my mother forsake me, the Lord will take me up. I have not time here now in introductory manner to follow further along these familiar break-

downs of human life, and see them reenforced by
faith; but this is my preachment beyond and
through them all: "I will say of the Lord, He
is my refuge and my fortress: my God; in him
will I trust."

In daring to name some of the elements in the
man God needs, there seemed to be a presumptuous liability. We doubtless will be liable to
the blame of presumption in noting the qualities
of the God man needs. God is God, and there is
with him no variableness, neither shadow of
turning. I would not seem to be setting any
human requirements toward God's character. I
am only to seek now the evidences of the fact
that where humanity falters it finds God ready.
We fail into divine help.

Colonel Robert G. Ingersoll made much capi-
tal in attention a few years ago with a phrase he
coined: "Did God make man, or man make
God?" He was answered oft and fully, and,
indeed, the phrase itself was made one of the
most effective of all his answers. It, however,
caught a popular attention, and many easy
thinkers let its sarcastic interpretation silence
their religious desires. What I desire in this
inquiry now to do is to find where God has ful-
filled the needs of human life, and been a constant supplement to a faltering race. "God
shall supply all you need according to his riches

in glory by Christ Jesus." Someone long ago, in commenting on that fact, wrote well thus, "Man and God cannot remain apart, but tend toward each other by an irresistible necessity, for God would be the God of man, and man must be the man of God. We may restrain the tendency of things, but we cannot abolish the law of attraction."

I shall endeavor, in a reverent appreciation of God, to point out some of the things man needs to find in him. I shall dare to interpret the true need of man as a constant appeal to the Almighty. The popular conception of religion needs a marked change from a patronizing idea of God which has crept into our day through a false magnification of the importance of mortal welfare. The kind of a God man needs may not of a certainty be found by a careful consultation of his wants. Our needs and our wants are, often in the most common things of life, very far apart. I have wanted much I never really needed. I have needed much I never wanted at all. I shall not be surprised to find that there will be discovered places where that which I want in my God, and that which I need, are very different, and need, not want, is the safest basis of my judgment.

God forever watches for the place of human falter. He notes with solicitous care the extreme

of our endeavors, and there with his infinite
interest welds his own arm to our tasks. I confess to a liking for that. It sounds like religion.
It refreshes my soul. It quickens my last
strength. What God can do for me! Who would
ever dare to go boastfully about the earth listing the things he himself could do? We all carry
too much sorrow of falterings to lift any proud
professions. In the humbling consciousness of
our own weaknesses, we would express our grati-
tude for his supplemental interest. After all, I
only want the God I need. I endeavor to maintain my independence as far as I can go, knowing that to be an all too short way. What I can
do alone, however, I am determined I will do.
There is a saving independence which God has
planted in my soul. It was given me in expectation that inside that range I would thoroughly
work out my own life. When I was a boy I
prayed as honestly as a boy can pray (and there
is no more honest prayer ever heard from this
earth than a child's prayer). I prayed to be
rich. I knew a man who had a team of horses
and a carriage. I knew a boy who had a bicycle.
Those folks were rich folks, as I thought then.
We had no horse and carriage. I could have no
bicycle. But these things I wanted. I lifted a
perfectly honest prayer that I might be rich, and
that prayer was focused upon horses and car-

riages and bicycles. But the prayer never was answered. I became a Methodist preacher. God is not at the beck of poor folks here on earth to hand them riches. That is their own business. Poor folks are getting rich all the time, and it doesn't matter much anyhow. God makes folks capable of riches, and leaves the collection to them. I honestly believe now that if I were not so busy being a preacher I could go and get rich. God has made a world ready for that. He has stored mountains with yellow gold. He has hidden diamonds under the sands. He has poured great waterfalls down over the rocks. He has girded the hills with iron. He has planted fertility across the great valleys. Go there, man, and get rich. You can do it yourself.

In that stands clear the reason the manhood of our day is so hard to reach religiously. It is a long way to human need to-day. Man is sufficient with a very far-flung horizon now. Our grandfathers came to their sense of need on a much shorter route. They spent themselves quicker. They had no command of nature's genii, as we do. When their arms failed, they were at their limit. We carry dynamite and steam and electricity. It takes the patience of death itself to tire us down now. Need comes to us on a very slow foot to-day. I have seen recently strange comparative maps of our country scaled to the abilities of to-day, yesterday, and the day before. One was a large map scaled to the slow movements of the pony express of our grandfathers. Another was a much smaller map scaled to the comparative efficiency of the great express trains of to-day. Another was a tiny outline of our country scaled to the new air mail route bringing our two coast lines, but a day's journey apart. Men are proud in ability now. It is a long, long way to helplessness. Many men do not seem to see that they ever will get where they will not be sufficient. Still the patient plan of God abides the day. He knows this great manhood, proudly working itself out on this wonderful world will at last stand upon its own crumbling edge unsatisfied. All he needs to do is to just stand back farther and wait. Things may absorb us in the imperfect conceptions we proudly hold. God can wait, and wait he will, until man at last shall sit conscious of his need, even though that day be with a completed world in his lap.

There are two things I wish to say about man's God.

1. Man needs the God he needs. "Lean not on thine own understanding," is a well-authorized injunction which man finds hard to practice, and refuses to try until he has tested his own

strength to its breakdown. There was a pathetic little news item in my paper one morning, giving the account of the drowning of two young men in a northern lake. They had been blown from shore on a large cake of ice that broke away under the strain of a northwest wind. Their peril had been noticed by a woodsman who was on the shore within sound of their cries. He got a skiff, and dragging it to the edge of the ice-field, rowed out and rescued the imperiled youths. On the way returning to shore, in that confidence which came over them as they had escaped what they counted their real peril, a sudden squall capsized the skiff throwing the three men into the water. Their rescuer clung to the upturned keel of the boat till help arrived, but the two young men did not appear again. How impressive the incident with the fact that just when we have settled ourselves into confidence built about our own strength we have fallen! The sea of life is run through with sudden squalls, and unexpected currents that compel the oft-capsized sailors to look for God. Failure may be a little farther on for us to-day compared to our fathers. But what comfort is to be found in comparative failure? What matter distance and time to such a fact? Failure is what I despise. It is not the difficulty of success that drives me. It is not when or where I

44308

fail that troubles me. What care I how hard the
way that leads to the goal, if I can but make the
goal. It is that I shall actually fail that haunts
me. Comparison in failure carries no comfort.
If I am on an infinite ocean, I simply cannot
swim it. That being sure, I had as well drown
just where I am as a mile farther yonder. It
would save the struggle beside. Men have been
swimming the English Channel of late. Many
have failed bitterly. But some have found favor-
able wind and tide and wonderful endurance,
and have actually made the whole distance. An
uncrossable sea, however, whose horizon forever
falls back, had as well swallow my little body
here as a mile or a hundred miles, or a thousand
miles farther out. It is that uncrossable fact
that reduces every failure to sameness. That is
the peculiar place and sense in which I need God
in my life. The philosopher has brought me in
my mental processes to find out that I am capable of aspiring after ultimates, but am unable
to attain them. That is the make-up of the
strange contrariety we call human life. "I shall
be satisfied." Satisfied? Yes! answers the
Scripture. And then with that divine appreciation of that human hunger it seeks not to quiet,
but bids to continue, it flings the danger point of
stagnation called satisfaction far beyond reach
by prescribing divine bounds thus—"When I

awake in his likeness." That's safe. We cannot climb up to God, but God we must have. Plato, more effectually than all the philosophers, has put this truth at the extreme limit of his best endeavor with a declaration that the finite cannot cross the gulf of the infinite, the infinite must step out of its infinitude down to us. God must stoop down to man. It is the reality in that fact, and the great unfulfilled ambition in man which reaches beyond his ability, and discloses thus to us the kind of a God we need. That humanly impossible distance which runs on from our faltering feet and loses its tracings over behind the stars has forever made mankind feel about in the darkness for his God.

This fact explains Babel. Strange story that. To me no more pathetic story was ever written than the story of Babel. Poor little troubled men, running eagerly about with stone and mortar to build up a way to God. Build it high! Oh, build it higher and higher. It is never high enough. Hurry, men; you have not stone enough yet. More stone! More stone! How the workmen cry. Mud! Mud! Mud! Hear the masons calling! Sweating at their building in the blazing fields of Shinar. What a huge, pitiful, crude, but awfully convincing monument to the absolute need of man for God is that ancient pile of stone. It was that unquenchable determination

of man to bridge out the distance between earth
and heaven. How far is it from earth to heaven?
Surely, I can span it somehow! I will get me
up there some way! I am bound to get above
myself! God let them build. Build the tiny
tower no matter how high. Height measured by
masonry meant absolutely nothing. Build it
up! Maybe on days of low-sweeping clouds the
topmost stone can reach a wreath of cloud. But
this that building man must come to know, and
maybe Babel helped him find it out, for the same
thing is being forever worked out in experience:
When he climbs at last upon the highest stone he
can raise, and lifts his hands there toward
heaven, he is not one inch nearer God than he
was in the dusty field in Shinar. The God I
really need keeps out of the reach of all such
puny efforts. Babel is no strange story. It
was simply that day's edition of a very common
human experience. Man has always sought to
make his own way to God. The same story is
being built out again to-day. We think we are
wiser, and are using different material is all.
The effort is the same. The rampant intellec-
tualism of the hour is but a modernized Babel.
We are not out on the plain of Shinar shouting
mad orders to overstrained laborers. But we are
just as certainly and just as earnestly engaged
in the same hopeless effort, as ever were those

strange yet familiar workmen of Babel. We are trying to build us up a way to God.

O man! the God you need, is not One who sits over beyond an infinite gap, which separates humanity from divinity, and there awaits your impossible climb. You must face the other way if you would find the truth. It is shorter from the infinite to the finite, than it is from the finite to the infinite. God can reach across. You cannot make your way into the impenetrable shadows. Your compass fails you. Your polestar fades from the blackening heavens. We need a God, who will step out of the infinite, and putting at our disposal his love and guidance, will lead us tenderly but safely as a shepherd leadeth his flock.

2. The second qualification which must repose in man's God is that he must be able to forgive him his sins, and grant him the consciousness of righteousness. That is humanity's supreme need. Of all the words the preacher is ever called upon to say, none is so vital as the word that will declare effectually the fact of an open way from sin to forgiveness. That is the message all other messages are to be used to get more efficiently proclaimed. After a preaching experience reaching across thirty years, and contacting with life from the more remote farming regions, and smallest country villages, all the

way along the gamut of experience into the most
strenuous sections of congested city life, I am
ready to say there is no message the world wants
to hear as eagerly as the old, old gospel, that God
forgiveth human sins and does cleanse mankind
from unrighteousness. It is a necessity in the
God of this race of ours.

The Bible is saturated with that fact, and
presents eloquent examples everywhere that keep
its message abreast the needs of a sin-struck race.
He forgiveth my sins! I thank God for the personal consciousness of that preachable fact of
my faith. The world with all its wonderful
advancement has never outrun that need, and
never will. It matters not how rich we pile our
fortunes, or how cultured we train our brains
and manners, or how penetrating for facts our
scientific research shall become, man will never
work himself beyond the profound need of a
divine forgiveness of sins. One of my very best
personal friends, a man of great influence in the
world of business, one who commanded millions
of money, and possessed secured resources that
fortified him against all worldly anxiety, said to
me one day as we were talking as friends in his
office: "There is just one thing in my life I
regret. I would give all I have if I could wipe
out that regret. Of course I believe a man can
be forgiven by God, but what is he to do with

himself? That great regret stands ever before me." I told him, just as unqualifiedly as I could find simple words to say it with, that I had full faith in the meaning of the fact that God did forgive sin. It would be impossible for me to worship, or to imagine a God of a race, such as we are, who did not forgive sin absolutely. It is fundamental necessity. This world cannot be moved to salvation by preaching reform, though the preachment of that was never so diligently done as it is being done to-day. You cannot whittle the race into a figure of acceptable form, by brilliant endeavors of poetry, ethics, and art. All those things are good, and much to be desired. They do not, however, reach the real trouble. There is good authority written down to give us a warrant to say that it doesn't help a grave much to whitewash it. What the grave needs is a resurrection. The church of Jesus Christ must hold out clear and bold and without any excuse in qualification, the primary fact we know in our God toward all human sin. Sin is the world's troubler. It is in separating itself from sin our race has found its possibilities in service. Evidences of this high experience are to be found all along the ever-ascending trail that marks the way we come from sin to holiness. We cannot think of the God man needs knowing man as we all do know him, who would fail us

belief—that she had not a friend in all the world.
She did not blame anyone for the fact either.
She agreed. She had no case to offer. No one
had any faith in her. The whole town of Sychar
knew how bad she was, and without dispute left
her in her badness. They had not met Jesus
about that town, however. One day he came.
He had faith in that woman. He took time and
went out of his way, and out of the restraints of
accepted prejudice to go and tell her so. He said
to her, as he measured her possibility of recovery
on toward a real usefulness she could render,
"Woman, go and sin no more." If Jesus Christ
could believe that that poor sinful creature
could go on into a good life, then she too could
certainly start anew with faith in herself. And
she did so.

Thank God for the contagion of faith, which
God's faith in man has enabled man to keep in
himself. The other night after I had finished an
address before a session of an Annual Confer-
ence in a large Eastern city, a man asked me if
I would allow him to take me to the railroad
station where I was to meet my train. I had
closed my address with an account of an impressive salvage God had made out of an abandoned
wreck. This man, who asked me to ride with him
did so in order to tell me the story of his own
life. Ten years ago he was a useless, yea even

a dangerously broken man. He had been a saloon keeper and a drunken wreck. No one had faith in him. He had with systematic regularity practiced his hypocrisy of promises, and collected everything he could collect on declarations he never meant to keep. God, however, did have faith in him; and it was that seemingly simple but fundamentally powerful fact that did at last build a new life into that man, and made him, what now for over ten years he has been—a positive aggressive force for righteousness in that city.

Man's God does forgive his sin, and cleanse him from unrighteousness. Sometimes God has swept away every trace of our wrongdoing, and there remains no more of it in this life. Suppose any of us got exactly what we deserve! There are some miracles I am very sure. Men have gone to the very breaking edge and not gone over. Others have gone over the brink in dreadful ruin. Beside the terrible havoc sin hath wrought there be some who cry that God is implacable, and has excepted them from grace. He has not! He has not! I would preach that to every life everywhere. I want you to see the God I love, the God I know we all need so much, who meets now, as he has met across long centuries, of all human sin could scrawl across experience, penitence at the Cross of Christ, and there by the alchemy of divine forgiveness the curse of sin is transformed. There are many who would, if they could, go again and stand at the beginning of life's journey. Who of us would not change some things we must recognize now as vital parts of life? Life is so rich a possibility that if it were the privilege of all who have tried it to be given the chance to improve upon what they had done, there would be no conclusions here. While we cannot go back to begin anew, God has wonderfully provided for all this longing after better things in the cross of his Son our Saviour. When we stand there in faith beside the multitude who have there found life anew, and Peter and Paul, and Mary Magdalene, and that increasing company where life in every failure sin can render has been recovered—there we will realize that the Saviourhood of the Master is inclusive enough for us all. Man's God finds most perfect expression in Jesus Christ.

VII

UNEXPECTED BLESSING

"Who passing through the valley of Baca make it a well."—Psa. 84. 6.

I LIKE that verse. It is one of the refreshing passages in the Bible which brings impressively to me that strange richness of God's Word whereby it always seems to say more than it says. I quote this phrase often. I keep it in my constant reference memory. It is one of the places I like to stop to rest my sometimes tired way. This sentence to me is always full of surprising and happy meanings.

The valley of Baca. That is a dry old place. It sounds dry, and parched, and dust-choked. Whoever named that place knew how to match words against conditions. I will need no guide to tell me when in my goings I am come to Baca. The name is sufficient. I will know it. If I were asked to name a dried-out, hopeless route to somewhere, I would call it "Baca." The Baca route! Who would ever travel there?

I think of some of the ways through the dried deserts I have seen. I have seen coming in from those sanded ways the long, weary, swaying cara-

vans of camels. Out of the desert. What fine
tread of thanksgiving came along with them then,
as they found again the first green carpets of
grass to tread upon! Earth holds no more
wearying place than the waterless wilderness.

You who have driven your automobiles across
our continent do not forget that trying run you
had to make through the desert. Baca! You
closed every window in your car. In grim determination, and without talk, you drove as hard
as your old engine would respond, through that
dreary region. How the dust crept in! How
your face burned! How the hot way shimmered
before you there! When the great transconti-
nental trains pass through the wretched place,
they almost seal the coaches. They even pull
down the curtains of the windows. They use the
electric lights. They turn the whirring electric
fans against the determined climate. The porter
keeps up a constant crusade against the dust that
filters in at every crack. The Baca Route! No
one ever advertises that. Everyone desires to
escape it. They advertise in artistic and attractive pictures, Yellowstone Route, Columbia
River Drive, Yosemite! These they picture with
refreshing streams, and lovely waterfalls, and
fresh green trees. If ever they paint on the poles
along our way a legend, "Baca Route," we will
make a detour.

All that seems easily couched in what the psalmist introduces his sentence with—"Who passing through the valley of Baca"; and we are wearied already in the reading. Then the great sentence is finished in all the fine declaration of religious hope in contrast to whatever weariness life may bring—"Maketh it a well"; Baca and a well are the two balancing terms. Maketh Baca a well! How refreshing the very thought. Give me a cup! No, never mind that formality. I am too thirsty for a cup. I will drink out of the dripping, cool old bucket, and tilt it over on the edge of the cool, damp well-curb, and drink from the wet edge of the gentle curve of it, that is too big to get between my thirsty lips; so I must feel the water that runs down my cheeks and drips from my face. Oh, that is what I call a drink. It may not be sanitary in these sanitary days of ours, but that is not the matter of this talk now. I am talking about getting a drink when I am absolutely thirsty.

A well in the valley of Baca. Did ever a well look so good? Was ever a well better located? I never get particularly stirred to enthusiasm over a well that is found just beside a lake or a river. Where there is water abounding a well loses its meaning. I remember the instruction I have received in reading for the best method of obtaining water when on a camping expedition. I am told to dig a hole in the sand near a stream, or a lake, and am assured that the water that seeps into the hole I have dug will be fit to drink. I presume the instruction is good. I have tried it. But when I watched the clearing waters in my little sand-hole I was not genuinely thirsty. It is a well, struck in the midst of the dry, hot desert place that carries all the fine meaning of a well of water.

I thought I would fix in my mind the exact location of the valley of Baca. I have seen many very dry routes in Palestine. In fact, that is one of the most impressive facts in any traveling one can do in that part of the world. It is a dry country. Dust is common. Wells are few. Springs are fewer. Dust clings heavily to scant vegetation along the roadsides. There is no sight to me so depressingly dry as the sight of trees and grass and corn, and even the weeds along a dusty road, all choked with dust. Where is the valley of Baca? I turned to my map of that familiar land and could not find it. It pleased me to find that no one could locate it. I was glad, because I know where there is a place that is just like Baca sounds. I was glad no one had ever surveyed any one particular somewhere out, and that therefore such a place could still be real to each and every one of us. Don't you remember Baca? Of course you do.

The revised version has changed this word in the text, and written it in perhaps more correct phrase, but in the extravagance of prosaic accuracy. It is written correctly thus, "Passing through the valley of weeping." None of us need an atlas to locate that bit of geography. We know. The great big fact that stands out clear in this phrase is that very much of the real story of human life has never been charted. Who can set down the geography of the human soul?

The geography of Palestine was influenced much by human experience. Blessed fact indeed to be written across hills and valleys. Those folks named places after great spiritual events. Events are human rather than racial, therefore much of their geography has leaped beyond their country, and has come to be part of a world language. The geography of Palestine is a strangely significant spiritual guidebook. "On Jordan's stormy banks I stand." What a human fact that is! A whole world has separated that particular bit of Palestine geography into one of its favorite expressions toward death. "Out of my stony griefs, Bethel I'll raise." When one interesting day I stood on a quite barren, stone-covered hill, and they told me I was standing at Bethel, I could not but feel that greater fact of Bethel that had gone building great altars out of stony griefs across a whole world which was to me more impressive by far than that little hill in Palestine. It was a human experience written in geographical phrases. To me that spiritual Holy Land, which has thus been made to be familiar location to a whole world, is of greater influence in the human story than is the mere surveyed geography itself. It is not the mountains round about Jerusalem that are great. They are, in fact, little hills. We have mountains in our own great West that go trampling on those Judæan hills, as giants upon anthills. But, the world has spiritualized those little hills, until they rise expressive of infinitely more than any mere mountain could possibly become. "As the mountains are round about Jerusalem so the Lord is round about his people." The whole world possesses this geography. Jordan is in the song of humanity.

The man who has been disappointed in his maps because he could not point out there the location of Baca, has doubtless been looking at too small a map. Baca is bigger than geography. Baca is as big as the human heart. I am not in this familiar verse of Scripture seeking for a location where may be found mere hills that are dry and desert places that lie toiling in death through narrow valleys. I am looking for the genuine matters of the soul. I am trying with geographical terms to write into your keened interest the fact that our religion can produce a life that can pass through the valley of Baca and make of it a well. We must not allow the valley to overwhelm us. We must transform the valley. Any valley. Even Baca.

That is what our religion should be forever doing for each of us. If I could but know the whole story of any assembled audience anywhere among us, I could easily lead to attention there the triumphant demonstrations of this fact. That was exactly what David was singing about in this fine song. He had been watching the people as they came toiling up the climbing roads that lead to Jerusalem, where they were to worship. "Blessed is the man . . . in whose heart are the ways of them. Who passing through the valley of Baca make it a well; the rain also filleth the pools. They will go from strength to strength, everyone of them in Zion before God . . . appeareth. I had rather be a door-keeper in the house of my God, than to dwell in the tents of wickedness."

The fact I would pursue for your attention here is that the soul who believes in God will change difficulty into blessing, and in unexpected places there will break forth before them the evidences of richest joy. Life with God is superior to circumstances. Wells in deserts. That is where wells are at their best. What a truth this

is to preach to a world such as we are living in!
Folks are famished in Baca. They are discouraged, and downcast, and surrendered, and
broken. Not so the soul who trusts God. He
is the God of Baca. Did ever any well anywhere look better than the one in Baca? How
refreshing its water! One nice, cool well in
Baca seems better than a river in the valley of
plenty. I have heard the old soldiers tell of the
wonderful "Miracle Spring," that broke out in
the dry, hard ground in Andersonville Prison.
Few incidents of our whole Civil War, made a
more profound impression upon the soldiers. A
good, cool well in a dry place. I remember a
well on the farm of a friend of mine in Kansas.
I remember it because it remained a refreshing
well in a distressing time. We were having a
drought. Everything in the country was drying
and withering away. The great fields of corn
had turned yellow and died. The grass in the
pastures was dead. The water in the ponds on
the prairie and in the great pastures had all
dried up. The last deep tracks in the mud, made
by the thirsty cattle as they had waded there to
suck out the last drops at their watering places
had dried into hard sun-baked earth. Great
cracks had opened in the parched ground. The
rivers had ceased to flow. Only in the deeper
holes along the river's way, could water be found

to quench the cattle's thirst, and the farmers would drive their cattle along the dusty roads twice each day to the pools in the drying river beds to drink. That is the remembrance in my life that comes rushing back to me when you talk about Baca. It sounds just like that dreadful drought. But my friend had a deep well. It was not only deep, it was cool. It never had failed. We would come sweating and panting through the sweltering days up to that wonderful well, and drink, and drink, and drink; and then bathe our hot faces in the cool crystal water. That is when a well is a well.

That is what God's promise is. A well in Baca. We are not exhorted to endure Baca. We are promised that one wonderful day, if we don't falter, we will be delivered from it all. O Baca, Baca, how hard you are! But, God helping me, I hope some day to survive you! That is not the program of our faith. That is cheap talk in the face of the intention of our great deliverance. There are things we must bear, and those things we will not seek to avoid. They shall indeed make in each one of us a far more exceeding and eternal weight of glory. But above and beyond all that, there remains a fairer truth. I am trying now to find a clear word, against an all too common habit among us, which seeks comfort from difficulty and sorrow, by vague unrealized promises that such things cannot last forever. It is the comfort which inheres in mere desperation. Our religion is not foundationed on desperation. We have a better comfort to offer than one which in grim necessity seeks to keep alive and wait. If we can but get past Baca! It will be but a desperate chance, but there is a possibility we may hold out. That is not the note of our faith. It does not carry the confidence in God I feel.

> "Be still, sad heart, and cease repining;
> Behind the cloud the sun's still shining.
> Thy fate is the common fate of all,
> Into each life some rain must fall,
> Some days must be dark and dreary."

That is doubtless good poetry. I would not set myself against literary judges who long since have given that verse its undisputed place in our literature. It is the argument, not the poetry, I object to. It is a passive attitude. I know it will rain. To all that I am agreed. But with that admission it does not follow that I am compelled to stand unprotected in it. There are several things I can do. I can even get under a good roof. I can get an umbrella. I can even have a genuine good time in the rain if I so desire. I have done so. There are many interesting possibilities in a rain, other than to be overwhelmed by sadness. I don't intend to be

utterly rained out, just because that little poem
is pretty and submissive and sad. I will nego-
tiate the dark, damp day. The religion I profess has a message for every hard place in life.
It goes forward expectantly into those hard
places determined to plant deliverance there.
To put a well in Baca is a far better policy than
to hope to merely struggle through it somehow.
I like to believe that we can actually sit down
in Baca and make it comfortable. My Christianity would bring all a whole world's misery,
and suffering and sorrow and loss, right up to the
judgment of this heavenly optimism. There is
a much better program for Baca than to wait
it out. I am called to a refreshing, optimistic
interpretation of every difficult thing. Christianity would set a bright hope in the midst of
every darkening gloom. We must furnish the
world a positive deliverance. We are not to
exhibit the spectacle of a famished soul, half
dead from thirst, and coming through at last,
dust-covered and crawling up to the distant foun-
tain that is the final end of all our dogged
endeavors. I would gather instead here the fine
religious fact that this present-day life is not
merely to be endured, and at last worn out and
compelled to end with the scant comfort that
after while there will be a good time, but that
we have a positive message of deliverance for

now. We have a program for Baca. We propose relief in Baca, not merely beyond Baca. There is a refreshing assurance in being told that, after all, when we are in trouble we will find the help of our faith, not merely in lifting up our eyes to far-off hills that raise their purpling heads out of a distant future, but, rather, that in the very heart of this present moment we are to know its full meaning. Baca can be made a well. That is preachment for to-day. Folks need that now. Who will write hope brightly across this present-day situation? That is the need whose readiness lures to passion every preacher who really senses the meaning of our faith to-day. Victorious life every day! Victory everywhere! Just what the particular issue of any particular day may be is not a qualifying condition. It may be sunshine or cloud. It may be war or peace. It may be joy or sorrow. It may be Beulah or Baca. Whatever it be, this faith will set a well in its midst. Not even death itself can dry that well away. There is nothing that can stop such hope. I expect victory in death. I am not merely looking for a bright heaven after death. I am confidently expecting complete victory in the very midst of death itself. I want a well in that valley. I want to tune my song to triumph there. Oh death, where is thy sting! Oh grave, where is thy victory! That is the present usefulness of my ministrant faith. That will make Baca refreshing.

I am trying to find some word and phrase now that I may shout my confidence to all men, that our offered experience is such that no possible condition can arise that will not yield to our religion if rightly put. This is the way through, says our faith. Go on, man! Go on, woman! Go right on! You must go, and go alone, too. It is indeed weird going from one world to another. Vast multitudes have already gone. We who just this to-day are marching past the review stand are but a squad of the vast host already gone. Most everyone is dead. None can show us the way. All the steps of those ahead of us are rubbed out. Not a footprint before us. No trail blazed in this strange human dark. Nowhere can you think out such startling contrast as that between the uproar of this plunging world and the dense silence of the close beyond. I have been in oriental cities, and been impressed with the sudden quiet that comes on with the night. It seems almost as though by one common signal the quiet of the night comes down. But there is nothing we can dream out in comparison to the muffled silence death throws about us all. Yet we have reason to be of good cheer as we come up on this side of that strange venture. The way is upward. When the last moment comes, we shall find ourselves equipped in divine promise. One of the very noblest of dying men said just as he was being lost sight of here, "I am full of inexpressible joy, and go to die in perfect peace." John Wesley has been teaching the world how to die ever since he stepped on out and away, leaving to linger forever at the edge his last words, "The best of all is, God is with us." Many have gone out to death over paths of great suffering. Through flames, and through indescribable torture they have found a yet tolerable route, and written victory, victory, victory along its whole way. When they brought Doctor Taylor out to the commons where he was to add his death to the list of the martyrs, he said to those who killed him, "Thank God, I am at home here."

There may be among some folks these speculative days a troubled attitude, with agnostic tendency, toward what life beyond the grave will be. But the Christian hope, in its essence, is unchanged and unweakened. We go steadily forward to that "no-man's land" of our existence we call the grave, convinced that whatever there awaits us is certain to be eternally our best. An infinite love has ordered our way thus far. It will surely order our way out and to all that lies beyond. In the unfaltering trust of that great faith I want at last to die my death out.

Die, clear-eyed and unafraid. Die, even with blanched lips yet singing his praises. Die, even when my body is falling, yet with rising spirit, exultant and triumphant. I want to match right against that last and uttermost test of death all the beliefs of my life. That is what I call making the far end of the valley of Baca a well springing up unto everlasting life. That is the faith triumphant. It will change every valley.

To the positive practice of this transforming faith here and now I would call you each and all. Just where we are now. Maybe where business is troublesome. Maybe where losses are keenly severe. Maybe where you are dizzied and fainting with trials. Even where sorrow shall have hung its blackest pall. Right here and now we want a faith, a truth, a grace, a surety that will completely sustain us. I am so glad I can preach just such a promise. I only wish I but knew how to get it an attentive hearing where it is so much needed. Can we not find a new and refreshing interpretation of this fine word of David's song, to be sung now in interpretation by the Son of man, who walked through the vale of sorrow, and made it bright with his divine experience? He has put new meaning in all the long persistent hope of the wearied past. One great day, we believe, his passing through the vale of this world shall have proven completely triumphant, and where desolation, and strife, and sorrow, and sin now abound, there shall righteousness and peace meet together. The passing of Jesus Christ through this valley of Baca will be sure to make of it a well of living water.

I remember somewhere to have read the impressive incident of an old man who, when he learned that death was to be his next experience, turned to those who stood waiting his departure, and spoke of the weariness of his exhausted mortality. Then he said, "When I have gone, I want this old body laid carefully out there on the hill, beside the discarded bodies of my many friends, and I want you to lift a modest little stone over that resting place, on which these words from the Holy Book shall be cut: 'Being wearied with his journey.' " There in the little modest cemetery to-day leans a little marble slab over the old traveler's body. He was tired unto death! That is all the word they have lifted over him means. He had traveled through his full mortal tenure. Often the way was rough. Sometimes it was through suffering. Much was he in the dark. Many times he was utterly confused. There be many, oh so many now, who, like that wearied old man, wish honestly that the journey was actually done. "Wearied with the

journey," is no rare biography. It could well
be writ across a multitude. But that is not my
preachment now. I only dared to close this sermon with the perhaps well-known and a bit
oppressive incident, because it needs completion.
It is but fair to the great Book of God, from
which the wearied little word for the tomb was
taken, to say that it was not all there, and the
truth was obscured. We cannot write an immortal's story with only a mortal word. The whole
verse from which the old man took but a part
to word his weariness with, has a lifting, hope-
filled finish to it. I am so glad it was not left
as the gravestone has it. It reads thus, "Being
wearied with his journey, He sat thus on the
well." Oh, let us never leave that out when we
seek from this verse an inscription for our outward journey. Really, the tired old man's story
was not finished at all in mere weariness. The
valley of Baca was never meant to be nothing
more. It is a wonderful place to plant a well.
The very fact of Baca is an appeal for a well.
There is available for every one of us a well
spring. It is accessible to every passing pilgrim.
Life can never run itself so weary as to fail this.
There will never be for you or for me a place
so hard that the way will prevent the presence of
genuine divine refreshing. He who will always
meet you will thrill you with an immortal vital-

ity and gladness. "The Lamb which is in the midst of the throne shall feed them, and shall lead them unto living fountains of water: and God shall wipe away all tears from their eyes," and passing through the valley of Baca, they shall find it indeed a well.

VIII

REST BY ESCAPE

"Oh that I had wings like a dove! for then would I fly away, and be at rest."—Psa. 55. 6.

THUS sighed David, one heavy-hearted day of his, when escape seemed to be the ideal way to rest. I would fly away. Away! Anywhere but here. What I want is to escape. A winged route looks the easiest of all. I would get away. I wish I could fly. Surely somewhere else than here is ideal. I am sick of here.

The king psalmist is talking in familiar language when he sighs thus. It needs no interpreter to explain obscure phrases in such talk. We know this yearning for the escape to somewhere other than our own familiar and wearied place. How often I have longed to escape! Heart sick! Borne down by the long, hard, monotonous strain of life; tired of the pull, we drop our worn hands and sink into a welcome seat and sigh: "I wish I could get away from all this. If I but owned an island in some south sea, where weather was always mellow and mild, I would get on that island and forget the whole world. I don't know how I could ever get to it, but if I had the wings of a dove, I surely would not stay around here. I would at least fly away. I would find rest by escape. Where I have to live is unbearable. My task is crushing. My burden is intolerable. My strain is too much. What I need is escape. Oh for wings!"

Look at that foolish dove sitting there on the low roof of my house now! What does any dove, full rigged with a good pair of wings, want to sit around such a place as this for? I don't understand doves. A whole world is before them. Where could they not go? Yet here they stay, winter and summer, just sitting around and flitting around this weary place where I live. There goes one now! Surely he has found this place out and is outward bound. I start to wave him farewell, and he settles down on another low roof. There the whole flock goes! It looks like a migration of doves. They wheel in broad circles round a steeple, and settle back again on the same roof. Doves don't seem to have sense to match wings with. Wings are surely made to get away with. Think where doves could go. There is Florida! Every time the cold breath of winter snaps at my shrinking body, and I shiver under my close-drawn wraps, I look in amazement at doves in such a climate. There is Greenland! Every time the driving heat of August's perpendicular sun smites me, I look out in disgust at the doves still here. Wings of a dove, owned and controlled by a dove, seem all out of place to me. Why equip him so if he is content on so narrow a plot? He can find full joy in a city block. He could easily walk the whole round of his little going. It does seem his wings could be given to someone who would set out on a genuine journey somewhere. As I feel just now I surely would furnish such pinions a full test of flight. I would fly away.

I called a friend of mine, who is an expert flier, and asked him how much wing spread was necessary to carry a man. He said: "We call twenty square feet of wing a man-carrier." Twenty square feet! A dove's wings would be strained to a whirring flutter to carry my gloves. That startling whir of a partridge in flight is made by the extra effort of wings too small to sustain the weight, and thus compelled to beat in rapid succession at the sustaining air. A seagull, with light body, has a wonderful wing. He can glide on a breeze by the skill of his calculated position. Wings of a dove! You would be worse off than you are now, for now you know you cannot fly, and that is often the very heart of contentment. Compulsion will often conscript you to your task. I can't get away. I might as well go to work.

One of the commonest aims of my prayer has

long been that I might be saved from that uneasiness which comes from seeking rest by escape. There is so much more real heroism and genuine satisfaction in working out my rest in my place, wherever it may be. I want to prove myself right here, wherever that here may be. Location in geography has nothing whatever to do with this problem. I do not want escape. It is not climate that heals. The real rest of soul and life cannot be found by escape, but, rather, by victory wherever life is lived. Wings? No, no! What we need is a stout heart, and steady feet, and patient endurance, and tireless endeavor. Fight it out; don't fly away. Never mind about wings. Look to your feet.

One of the great arists has given us a most beautiful picture inspired by contemplation of this verse of David's. The famous king is shown sitting on the roof of his great palace just as evening gathers toward darkness. He is all alone. There is no crown on his head. He is a man now, with all thought of his kingship laid aside. He is wearied. He has had enough upon his soul to weary any man down. His heavy locks of hair, falling across his shoulders, are turning silver, and hastened so by both age and trouble. After all, what advantageth it to be a king when sorrow comes? There is no escape in royalty. The palace cannot build out trouble.

Up the marbled stairs of the palace of the greatest king Israel ever had, trouble seemed to come
with persistent pursuit.   Yonder, under a
humble little fig tree, sat a simple husbandman
happy in his unpretentious place. His sons and
daughters were happy about him there. It was
a glad home. There was nothing on the heart
of that plain husbandman to bring him down in
sorrow. What is the advantage in being a king
anyhow?   That great heart-broken king of
Israel, whose life and home had been shattered
by sin, was longing for the plain, honest life of
a shepherd which he had given up just to be
a king. "I would be a better, and I am sure a
happier man, if, instead of having become a king,
I had but remained a poor, unknown, ruddy,
healthy shepherd, and had gathered the frost of
years on my simpler and untempted life as a
watcher of quiet flocks, and had never taken on
my heart the troubles of a kingdom and the sorrows its temptations have brought me!' As the
saddened memory of the king thus waited upon
him, a flock of pigeons wheeled about over his
head, and at last flew away behind the roofs
over toward the sunset. They seemed to whirl
into words the feelings that were struggling for
expression in his soul: "Oh that I had wings
like a dove!" I am sure he stood up to look
over the walls after the vanishing flock of fliers

as they flew, as he continued. "I would fly away." Away from all this I know to be so troubled and so trying. If I could but get away, I am sure I could be at rest. "Lo, I would wander far off, and remain in the wilderness. I would hasten my escape from the windy storm and tempest." We all know just how David felt. He has found a universal phrase here. He was speaking out of an individual experience, doubtless more bitter and disappointing and extreme than any of us will have to meet, and yet we need no explanation of his word. The route of escape he cried out for has set luring temptation to us all. The song of a king is tuned to the very same key as mine. I know that tune. To be sure, it surprises us just a little to find it coming from a situation wherein we have been led to believe comfort was spread at its softest. We have often thought that being a king was just the place we were sighing for. If I were king! Many of us have started the story of our deliverance from distress with those words. Here we are with so many handicaps at being just common folks that we have thought, had we but some good flying ability, to fly us out of this present unsatisfactory situation, we would certainly head straight for a throne. If I were king! If I but had a palace, and commanded an army! Oh if I but had horses and chariots, I would never think in so diminishing terms as dove wings. If I could but be saved from these little nagging things of a mere fight for a living. I weary at that. Merely holding my job. Merely supporting my family. Just the plain, doggedly persistent fights of my monotonous everyday life. I had always thought that if it ever became mine to wing away for rest from what I know life to be, I would go straight for a king's palace. But I hear this great king sighing for the same thing I want. Come along, King David; you can fly right along with the rest of us. We don't just know where we will ever be able to light, but we are seeking rest, just as you also are. Where shall we all go? "Ah, whither shall I flee for rest?"

It is because we have dared to try to write "rest" up against a some particular where of a place, that I am now in this somewhat strange manner trying to destroy that idea from our minds, in order to write a more genuinely religious fact in its place. We will never find rest by escape, but by genuine repose which abides within.

One of the most outstanding values of the Bible to this world lies in the fact that it deals with essential matters of character in universal manner. Particular incidents are forever being interpreted in human significance. The outstanding characters whose lives are woven into the great Book—the kings, prophets, poor men, cowards, heroes, sinners and saints—are so very much like all of us. The very same fights of weariness and discouragement with which we are familiar in personal experience, are written here in the experience of those whose lives have been God-noticed for the ages. None of us would ever have written the kind of a book the Bible is, had we been writing a book for the ages. We would have been more careful of our characters. When you write the stories of folks in books it is easy to leave things out. Sacred history will surely need characters of strange insight in conduct. We would have made our characters march undismayed through all conflicts because their eyes were on the certain outcome. We would not have written a very human story had we been asked to write a sacred book. There is so very much of the human that is separated from everything that is sacred we would disclose but little of it. But the Bible is strangely human. It is not afraid to be so. God is never perplexed. So divine is the Bible in its make-up, it is not afraid to be human. An impostor is so fearful he will be discovered he often overdoes the effect. A genuine character is never afraid of exposure.

One of the most human facts, any of us humans

know, is the fact of utter weariness of this world, which emboldens itself to utter carelessness as to whether it remain here any longer. We seek to escape. Whither shall I go? The Bible carries that human fact across many of its pages. Jonah wishes himself dead. Solomon with all his wisdom and riches and pleasures and influence, declares it all vanity. Moses, propelled by as great a heart as any human breast ever carried, cries out in genuine anguish of soul, "Lord, I am not able to carry this people alone; and if thou deal thus with me, kill me, I pray thee, out of thy hand, if I have found favor in thy sight, and let me not see my wretchedness." Elijah was as rugged and brave a man as our race has grown. There he lies under the juniper tree whose very name he has made symbolic with discouragement for all time. Job cursed the day he was born. Jeremiah has become proverbial in his outcry. Paul, never a moment daunted, and victorious amid everything life and death could conspire against him, cried out one day amid the conflict, that he might depart and be with Christ, which was far better. This is the universal trial of good souls who have had to fight with almost impenetrable stupidity in life. It is the bane of good men fighting pharisaism. The Bible has many sighs in it that well up from just such experience, and in every one it is sounding a condition familiar in the ordinary story of human life. God always runs his great Book familiarly close to us all. History in ordinary seems here set to divine meaning.

I want now to set square against the common experience of discouragement the great fact of genuine faith in God, and to declare my belief that with God escape is no route for rest. Short cuts of escape from the heroics of endurance are not found in the true tactics of trust. I would fly away. Where would you go? Well, I have not exactly decided upon my destination. It was not destination that was in my mind. What I had decided upon was that I must get out of here. Almost anywhere would be preferable to where I am. It is escape from, not whence to, that I am concerned with.

Rest is not a matter of location. There is very little geography in this great problem. I know how easily our difficulties take upon themselves a local flavor, and we come to believe a large amount of the fundamental troubles we sustain would be removed, if we could just find a better place. I am convinced that that false notion is the fertile ground from which springs a vast amount of life's dissatisfaction. Some day, after you have gone far in search of what you have come to call a relaxation, and have spent a whole day in recreation of the most approved

sort, and are coming back home wearied of body
and hence sure you must have found what you
went for, just drive on past your home and go
down into the congested section of the city,
where are the plain, crowded dwellings, the
grassless lawns, the barren porches, the absence
of everything you have come to count essential
to your plainest comfort. Drive carefully now,
for the streets will be crowded with little children, whose shouts and laughter are a genuine
music of the games they play with no equipment
other than playful childhood. Listen carefully,
for you will hear, if you catch what will surely
be there, the uncomplaining crooning of some
poor mother, who sits contented on a tiny porch
without a pillar, with no roof over it, rocking her
baby to genuine sleep in arms tired with work,
and yet content; and you, in all you have at your
well-equipped home, never sang a more tuneful
song of content. Rest is not a thing to go hunting for by migration. It is found in a state of
life, in a disposition and a principle of the soul.

The fine and preachable fact in the Christian
religion is, that we are to find our peace only in
our character. I am glad that fact is so. I am
glad I can preach it to the folks I know. It is
universal in its application, available for all
folks everywhere. We have no wings, and many
of us are even without carfare. We cannot get

away. We must stay here. There can come to us no help in the stories of other climates. Someone complained to me recently that the troubled doctor had informed him that he must get to some other altitude. The information was easy to impart, but the going could not be accomplished, and so the patient had to face the same old climate with the added handicap that he could not finance an information he possessed. We are living in a day when restlessness is seeking along every route to shift location for comfort. In the winter we have cultivated our desires to sit in the sunshine, and smell fragrant flowers. In the summer, we seek cooling shade under the evergreens growing along the fringe of winter to the north. The whole world is exploited for a changing ease. We seek to escape to ease.

I have a permanent message of religion. A fact of life that will defy surroundings or circumstances, a condition that will keep us warm in snowstorms, and cool in summer's glare. "There is a happy land, far, far away!" is the refrain of a desperation in a hope that holds on for deliverance. We have a better song thus:

> "Content with beholding His face,
> My all to His presence resigned;
> No changes of season or place,
> Can make any change in my mind.

The midsummer sun shines but dim,
  The fields strive in vain to look gay,
But when I am happy in Him,
  December's as pleasant as May."

So sings the soul that has found the supreme place of comfort in character. It is an offered peace that passeth understanding. We can live everywhere contacted with heaven, mountain top and valley's depth, tropics and arctics; heaven laves this whole world. What you cannot find by any migration, and what you cannot be deprived of by any location, you will find in the offered experience of trust in God. "In the world ye shall have tribulation: but be of good cheer; I have overcome the world"—so promises the Word. I shall therefore expect to realize in Him, and regardless of the where of it all, shall come to know the power and the purity and the repose which I have always longed for. The thing, down in my heart, which has ever allowed me to cry out, or which has stretched itself in uneasiness to escape to some other where, in order to find ease, I must now therefore be logical with in conclusion, and agree that it is cowardice and mistrust. I would fly away! What I desire cannot be had hereabouts. I must believe that such a cry for escape comes from a slinking idea that God will not, or cannot sustain us where we are, and hence we should shift location. Such a deduction does not breathe the spirit of defiance I like in genuine religion. I am not afraid that my place is too hard to trust God in. I expect him to sustain me here, right where I have come to think things peculiarly hard, and with an experience of such assistance I believe I shall find even more satisfaction than any other route to help could offer. Victory is better than escape. I had rather win than run. I will stand my ground with my faith unwavering. David's song was tuned to the deliverance of escape. The music is far better when tuned to that stronger phrase, "God is our refuge and strength, a very present help in trouble."

There is a divine deliverance which is to be obtained in the very midst of trouble. There is something extra satisfactory to feel comfortable in the midst of great liability. I appreciate the warm comforts of a glowing fireplace when I can hear the howling storm across the chimney and see through the windows the driving whips of snow lashing across the trees. I sat all night long, the coldest night I ever knew, with the shivering mercury huddled down to forty-eight degrees below zero, before a great wide fireplace, in the comfort of a lovely home, and talked to two of my most prized friends. The very thought of a howling storm whipped out always has brightened that night in my memory, and will never let it die out. Now, listen you to whom life seems to blow so hard and fierce at times, and in whose place the difficulty of the situation seems such a constant strain: "They that wait upon the Lord shall renew their strength." It does not say they shall find a better location. It promises strength for the place where they are. They shall mount, they shall run, they shall walk. Let come the storm! Here is victory in character.

These great delivering promises stand fast for us all. God has hedged our places with his assurances. "Yea, though I walk through the valley of the shadow of death, I will fear no evil: for thou art with me; thy rod and thy staff they comfort me." Why, then, should there ever leap up from my heart a cry to escape my place as a hope for ease? Why should I ever plan to flee? Dove wings, or railroads: I ask neither as a means of escape. I will stand my ground with faith in God. I have a confidence in what deliverance can be wrought out in me right here.

Recently in our prayer meeting we were telling each other our personal experiences with helpful hymns, and recording any incidents we had been impressed with, that clung around the interpretation of great lifting songs of our faith. It was helpful to us all. One incident was related as it has been told by Dr. S. Earl Taylor and recorded recently in a little book, *One Hundred and One Hymn Stories,* by Carl F. Price. Dr. Taylor was in India once when a total eclipse of the sun was experienced there. Many of the people were greatly disturbed by the strange event. Vast throngs, believing the sun was being swallowed by a great dragon, had hastened to their sacred river, and were there engaged in their most sincere religious services. As the darkness became dense the excitement of the great throng was impressive. The missionaries were looking down upon the people in pity from the windows of the Young Men's Christian Association building. Suddenly to their profound interest they heard rising sweetly and impressively above the murmur of the troubled multitude the strains of a song. The Christian natives had not failed to make use of the occasion. They knew about the eclipse, and standing right there in the midst of that which troubled and drove into a frenzy those darkened millions, those Indian Christians had tuned their song, and stood on the famous shore of the river so strangely worshiped by millions, and sang:

"The whole world was lost in the darkness of sin;
The light of the world is Jesus,
Like sunshine at noonday his glory shone in;
The light of the world is Jesus.

Come to the light, 'tis shining for thee;
Sweetly the light has dawned upon me;
Once I was blind but now I can see;
  The light of the world is Jesus."

The impression was overwhelming. God is able to deliver you. Let not fear seize upon you. It is no question of place. It is only a question of your relationship with God.

"In the time of trouble he shall hide me in his pavilion. In the secret of his tabernacle shall he hide me; he shall set me up upon a rock. And now shall mine head be lifted up above mine enemies round about me: . . . I will sing, yea, I will sing praises unto the Lord."

IX

MAKING FRIENDSHIP CHRISTIAN

He first findeth his own brother Simon, and saith unto him, We have found the Messias which is, being interpreted, the Christ. And he brought him to Jesus.—John 1. 41, 42.

MAKING friendship Christian. What an eternally important transformation that is! There is something so genuinely worth while in simple friendship itself, that the tragedy of Christian failure may easily lurk in the fact that we shall be content to allow our friendships to become no more than friendship. That is an illustration of the good becoming a substitute for the best, which will run into all our memories to awaken some incidents that will not be comfortable Christian meditation. To me as a Christian man, charged before God with the privilege of friendships, with many to whom I am sure my friendship has never been any more than mere friendship, I make this frank confession, that I look back across the all too lean years of my life in shame for the fact that I have done so very little with my friendships, when really they have always been and are now the most fertile Christian privilege available to me. It is a privileged

147

responsibility to have a friendship. My friends should be friends to my friends. The one great friend I know is this Lord of mine, whose I am and whom I serve.

A man's relationship to his friends, and his friend's relationships to him, must remain among the most critical judgments of his life. The friendships of a Christian that fail to carry through the offered doors of that fine relationship the natural solicitude of Christian interest, have most certainly failed with bitterest liability.

Let me tell you a story of my own failure that has followed me across the years, and is doubtless the prompting idea behind this sermon, and that I am willing to tell only because I do not believe it is a lone fact in my life, but will find parallel interpretation in the experiences of many others. In a little Western town on the prairie, where I began my ministry, lived a man with whom I became a fast friend. He was one of the fondest friends I had, and is to this day. Several mere incidents brought us together for acquaintance, and that acquaintance quickly ripened through our kindred affections into a lasting friendship. We had been married on the same day. We met each other the first time on the day we each brought our brides into that little village. A mutual friend gave a dinner for the four of us, and our two homes began their existence in mutual interest. My friend was not a Christian man, and, indeed, had never been a church attendant. For years he had never been inside a church, and had only been then at the funeral of a neighbor. Christianity had not any attention from him. A very interested friendship sprang up between us. It grew daily. Our homes were separated only by the street, and we became frequent guests at the tables of each. He began coming to church. He became a regular attendant; in fact, none was more regular than my friend. I held a special meeting in the winter, and a goodly number of people were converted and came into our little church. But my friend was not one of them. We hunted together often. We fished the little streams together. River and woods were to each of us real fascinations. We were easily friends. I moved from that village, and took a pastorate in another little town, so far removed that our friendship became dependent upon mere letters. A baby boy came to gladden his home, and he gave the boy my name. After I had been two years away, a quite remarkable revival swept through his community. A large number of people were graciously converted, and the little church was greatly revived. My friend was, however, not among them. He had become a character of influence, and failure to win him was a matter of genuine concern to the Christian people. He attended the services but was not moved. Many spoke personally to him, but he refused their invitations and gave no reason therefor. One inquisitive friend, a bit more insistent than the others, urged him to state some real reason for refusing to accept the invitation. He answered her in somewhat sensitive manner: "Don't ask me. I doubt the whole thing. I have felt that if Mr. Rice really believed it himself, he would long ago have insisted upon my acceptance of it, for we are the very best of friends. He never said anything to me about this matter." That stunning answer of the sought man, was sent to me on the first mail, and with it came an appeal to come once more to that little church and see if I could do anything to win my friend. You cannot know how those words of his hurt my soul. I felt as though the timidity of my young ministry had made it utterly fruitless. I had wondered very often about my friend, but never had I thought how essential it was for me, a Christian, to transform my privileged friendship into Christianity. I accepted the invitation, and went eagerly back to that little town. I tried to preach right into the face of such an accusation of failure as that, and it was hard preaching. I have never preached through a more difficult atmosphere in all my life, and atmosphere has much to do with preaching, as all preachers will know. I went personally to solicit my friend for Christ and beg his pardon for having been so poor a Christian friend. I stayed in his home. I prayed at his table. We talked by the hour. I led several others to Christian decision. My friend told me many times in explanation, that the answer he gave the urgent friend, about my failure with him, was only an effort to get rid of a request that had become troublesome. But that never satisfied me. I wrote him about it when I went home. But I have never to this day seen that fine friendship turned into Christian experience. I have always felt that I failed him as a Christian friend. Any friend would have done as much as did I. My being a Christian friend had not the least impression as distinguishment upon the relationship. He is to-day a business man in a large city. I am still an inefficient Christian friend of his.

How to make my friendship an open road to religion is one of the most serious questions I ever ask of my life. I have made bold to tell the story I have just told, a story that to me is crowded with tender and condemning memory of my own life, not merely to tell a story in illustration, for that I could easily find where there would be no hurt to me. I have told that story because I do not believe it is an exclusive experience of mine. I am sure it is a chapter in condemning neglect, that is written in the tender terms of the friendships of almost everybody. Our friendships should be our most vital and effective evangelistic appeal. Along the familiar ways of our most intimate relationships we surely should be ever finding appeals that would win those we are closest to, to the most genuine fact of our souls, our faith in God our Saviour.

I am persuaded that we have written the whole idea of evangelism in terms of strangeness these late years. The professional evangelist is a stranger to the community. He comes among us without the closer acquaintances we enjoy, one of another, and in the garb of that protective strangeness brings boldness into his urgency. It seems to be easier, I am wondering if we must admit also more effective, to appeal for religious decision where we are not closely known. This is a point of most serious meditation for the often much troubled pastor. Our acquaintances can be more boldly approached by us all on these great matters than our friends. Can it be true that a certain element of strangeness is an essential in evangelistic endeavor?

However you may answer that question in the light of present-day evangelism, I am sure that the original plan disclosed in the Bible would make every friendship of a Christian an open door for evangelism. If we were functioning aright in healthy Christian friendships, we would be preeminently Christian in our influence. This must not be interpreted into an obtrusive and objectionable use of our friendship. The true Christian influence must be attractive, and is not necessarily most effective when its aim has been openly disclosed. We have been troubled always by insistent folks who have lacked wisdom, and who have constantly carried Christian endeavor in a mistaken manner that was outstandingly repulsive. Christianity is attractive. Christian life is fascinating. Christian invitation is winning. Jesus Christ, in the supreme mission he came to perform in this world, has a right to a representation in each of us who profess him, to the most attractive life and conduct we can live. There is sure to be attraction in genuine Christian living. You need to be suspicious of your religion, if with it you are creating an uncomfortable attitude toward Christianity in those who know you best. It is no sign that you are living a high standard of Christian life because your presence is not sought by others. When God comes into a life it certainly should not therefore become stupid and repulsive. I am profoundly convinced, and convinced because I am so sure of the attractiveness of God, that the friendships of Christian people should be the most fruitful evangelistic influences that can ever be contributed from the human side of the transaction. There is a winning naturalness about friendship, which is the prime opportunity of our faith. Our religion should have right to a natural expression. There is always noticeable an immediate loss in appeal which comes from any apparent strain in seeming to be religious. Strange voices, strange manners, strange vocabularies, strange everything, as soon as the subject of religion is approached. We handicap our efforts with these unnatural things to all those who know us best, and actually yearn for a natural contact with us religiously. The gay, bounding heart of youth, whose carelessness of speech ripples with wit and humor, and whose light conduct seems to avoid everything that savors of the tread of foreverness, still carries deep there a conscious dissatisfaction, and yearns for something better and purer and higher, and is waiting and genuinely longing to be led; but it must be done without affectation. Youth sits often to wonder why the conversation of those from whom it is supposed to get counsel, is so very little turned atractively to real personal religion. That fact is, however, met much with the experience that there is a strange dread on the part of many Christian people to take up such a question.

There is a controlling conviction that the question of personal religion is a presumptuous matter for conversation. I do not know just why, for there are certainly these days a very few things which seem out of place in conversation. But personal religion is a subject for timid approach. I am afraid our fears are wrongly directed. A woman came to tell me of her experience in approaching the church and Christian decision. She had then been converted, and was not bringing me a critical report. She told me she had gone many times among the people she knew to be Christian people in hopes that someone would invite her to a Christian decision. She was not complaining, and said she, of course, had a perfect right to break in all by herself. Somehow she wanted someone to invite her. The truth of the whole matter seemed so very important that there could not easily be found a justifiable excuse for failure. I have wondered about her often since she told me her experience. I wonder if that conviction, born in her day of desire, has died from her own conduct in the day of her personal realization.

In this somewhat confidential manner now, I have sought to get attention to what I am convinced is the easy route to the greatest evangelistic movement the church has ever experienced. The whole proposition carries a condemnation upon us all, for there is a condemnation reposing in the sacred relationship we have with our friends, if it is not transformed religiously. I am likewise ready to face the reverse conclusion contained in all we have thus said, which is, that the blame for the lack of the coming of the greatest revival ever known in the church, lies in the fact that we have not cultivated our friendships to their religious conclusion.

There is a boldness which is easy to manifest in talking religion to strangers, but a tongue-tied timidity which possesses us before our friends. It cuts deep into my soul as a pastor (and I know in this I am speaking one of the keenest sorrows of the pastorate), to experience, as I ofttimes have, with what ease I can go away from my own familiar pulpit, and stir to decision those who are strange to me. I have refused many times to take up the work of evangelism to which I have been invited, a task which I have found so easily done away from home, and yet so difficult where I am a familiar character. Strangers can come among us and harvest religiously our own long-held friendships. Is strangeness a privileged influence? A young man came into our church service one Sunday morning recently. It was the first time he had been in church for a long time. He was a

stranger to every one there. His home was in a
distant city. He was strangely moved, and made
a personal surrender of his life to God under the
influence of the service. He told no one about
it. He determined as he left the church that on
the following Sunday he would return, make
himself known, and with public confession unite
with the church. He came, but was taken very
sick during the service, and was helped from
the room. A cab was called and he was taken to
the hospital. He died a few days later without
calling for me, and I only learned the facts after
he had been buried in his old home. To his
mother and sister who watched beside his sick
bed, he told the whole story and planted such
comfort in their souls that they wrote me the
full account of it, and described the service, and
the theme of the sermon, and asked that I send
them whatever I could of the sermon, for out of
it had been brought to that stranger, and to those
who loved him most, the hope of the world to
come, and the consolation for the sorrows here
known. Of course I thanked God for such good
results, but over beyond that stranger harvested
for him, I can still see those who know me best
who were unmoved, and are still. I am refreshed
by everyone who finds the way by the little
guidance I may be able to give, but the question
is forever rising before me, Why is it that many

who know me are unmoved? Can the fact that
they know me vitiate my sermon? Does friendship make ineffective my religious influence?
You, my friend! you unmoved now by my message to you, I assure you, that fact is one of the
most trying facts of Christian endeavor. I wish
I might get this difficult thing to say, said, in
words that will convey convincingly the full
meaning I want now. I firmly believe the reason
the conquest of the world for Christ halts so
very seriously is to be found in the fact that we
Christian people have never completed our
friendships religiously. We are not saving our
friends. The church is not actually reaching
religiously many of its very best friends. Can it
be true that we are satisfied with their friendship? Let me say that again, for it is one of the
most searching thoughts that has ever shot itself
into my Christian attention. Maybe we have
come to believe that friendship in itself is
enough. Maybe we are content to find folks who
have friendship for the church and its cause, as
a sufficient allegiance. They are good folks.
They are the very best people in the community.
They subscribe to all the collections. They support all the enterprises of benevolence. They
would never agree that the church should close
its doors. They attend the services. We have
just come quietly into the careless habit of allow-

ing that friendship to never make any fuller growth. We accept them as friends and call it enough. And that is a fatal neglect to both our friends and to our church. Friendship has presumptive rights. The friends of the church and of Christian people have the very first right of religious interest.

Christianity is tremendously responsible in its friendships. "He first findeth his brother," is the way our text puts it of a man who began at once to harvest his friendships. He first found his brother! Of course he did. He was sure of what he had found, and he first desired his best friends to partake of his good fortune.

There is a very significant meaning in the fact that the easiest man on earth to reach for a definite decision for a religious appeal, is the poor, outcast, abandoned, friendless man. Any offered hand to him is welcomed. He needs no argument. Theology presents no hindrance to him. His sins are open. He fears the judgment. He has no excuse to offer. The hard part about rescue mission work is not to persuade men to accept an offered salvation. That is the easiest part. The hard and sacrificing part, a part too for which so few are fitted, is to be constantly held with one's life against such abandonment as is always there. The work of the rescue mission is merely trying and not puzzling. The difficult task religiously is found when close friendship is approached for decision. We halt, we hesitate, we falter. We cannot find the right words. We become painfully unnatural. We know them so well. They know us so well. There can be no misunderstanding. These are our friends. Must it be admitted that close acquaintance is a barrier to evangelism?

The evidence of this peculiar evangelistic handicap is impressively revealed in the religious experiences of our homes. Folks seem strangely unable to win their own people to the faith. Parents are afraid of their children. They will talk with them, and endeavor to reason with them, upon all matters of ordinary conduct. But many parents whose hearts have been crushed, have confessed to me in the bitter agony that misconduct of children is so often bringing upon those who love them most, that the matter of religion has never been mentioned between them. Families are actually afraid of each other religiously. I listened one day to one of the most earnest Christian men I ever knew tell how he did the hardest thing he ever had to do. I had supposed, when he told us what he was to tell us about, that we were to hear of some great work he had set himself to do, that had cost him much money and time. He, however, surprised us all by telling us a simple story of how he had brought his courage up to the place where he could go personally to his own brother and ask him to give his life to God in Christ.

The halting evangelism of this hour in the Christian Church is due to the fact that we who call ourselves Christian to-day have not continued the effective policy of Andrew, which stands as one of the beautifully natural incidents in the earliest chapters of the establishment of the church. If, this hour, such a natural movement as this would become effective throughout the church, and boldly and earnestly lay Christian claim to all those who are already very near to us in vital friendships, we would see the greatest movement toward God the church has ever known. Think of that great company of men so near to the church, but only near. Men who attend regularly. Men who sympathize with all our purposes. Men who support the work. Men whose best friends are in the church. Men whose ears are constantly full of our testimonies of the power to save. Men who join their voices in our hymns of worship, and know as well as do we all the phrases of the creeds we repeat. Friends of the church, but we have not brought them to our Christ. They doubtless often wonder why it is so. They could now truthfully accuse most all of us, just as did my friend of whom I spoke in opening these remarks. They could point keen accusation at us for seeming to leave them out of the one real thing our religion is set to accomplish. We invite these friends of ours to our dinners, receptions, parties, everything but to our personal Saviour; and that is the very thing we maintain which must be accomplished in order to insure salvation.

I am trying in this unsermonic manner now to stand to attention against all of us what I shall dare call the condemnation of our friends. They may have heard from us the easy criticisms of what the church is doing. How easy that thing is to do! Our criticism is often eloquent, persistent, sure, fatal. Just now the church is suffering even before its best friends because it has so very much been given to a program of criticism. Let us shut off the criticism for a while now, and give full cooperation of an enthusiasm, born of our own genuine experience and a love of the great cause, and be honest with the cause of our Master in all our friendships. Let us go planfully to win the folks we know and love to our faith. Let us set enthusiasm's fire to our friendships for the sake of the true religion we profess. Let us keep our friendships sacred as our best opportunity of Christian service. Our churches should be the open doors, where the friends of Christ make constantly available the great friendship of Him who is "a friend that sticketh closer than a brother." The greatest Friend mankind has ever had should in the friendship of his friends find a recruiting place for the ever-growing company of those who are to be known as the friends of God. Every service of such a company of Christ's friends should be an invitation.

Several years ago a traveling salesman who had for years lived a careless life, and had tried, as he told me, everything the world had to offer, found himself on Sunday in a little village in Wisconsin. He sat in his little lonely room at the hotel and tried to list the things in which he had for long sought comfort and satisfaction. He was just as hungry and dissatisfied then, as he had ever been. He was sick of all that life had offered him. He decided to walk down the road and see if there was anything in so little a town as that, that would interest him. A church bell sounded across the meadows, and with the sound of it came a question to his conduct. He thought: "Well, I have tried everything but religion. I have no religious companions. My companions I have purposely made away from religion. The friends I have who are religious have never mentioned it to me. I do not, however, believe I am fair with life if I continue to leave religion an untried thing. I am going to church." All this had passed through his mind almost with the first clang of the little old rusty bell that had been ringing there for years, and almost every brazen clang it had made had died away in meaninglessness across the little hills. This man had not thought of going to church for years. He turned his steps toward that little church thinking to himself as he did so, "I wonder if they have anything to offer me." As he drew near the door he decided that if the preacher gave anyone a chance at that service to offer life to God he would do it. With such a resolve in his soul he found a seat near the door, and remained for the sermon. Who the preacher was he does not now know. What he preached about he does not know. Whether it was a good sermon or a poor sermon he does not know. The only thing he is sure of is that when the sermon was ended the preacher said, "Now if there should be anyone here present who wants this day to accept the Friend of sinners, and give God a welcome, the opportunity is open." My friend, who to-day is a fine and growingly successful man of business, said, "I am the man"; and up from that pew he arose, and walked down that aisle, and made a friendship with Jesus Christ. He has been a fast friend of his ever since, and has made friends of his friends. I have thought so often, since my friend told me that story of his life, and because he has become a so valuable man in the church, what a serious failure it might have been that day, had that preacher, a friend of our Lord's, failed to have called for those who wanted such a Friend. God has much to do with the preparation of a congregation. The Holy Spirit has much to do with the state of soul in which the listeners are. I would not be a faithful friend of my infinite Friend if I did not offer to you, my friends, this friendship of our Saviour and Lord.

Never can I lose the thrill from my soul which came to me as a heartbroken father handed me a little pocket Testament one day, and told me, between sobs, of having just returned from the burial of his last child, a son. He had once known a home of a happy family. "Now," said he, "they are all gone. I am a lone man, and even the Christianity I once enjoyed I have lost from my soul." He had come in to tell me a most tragic rebuke he had received. He was sitting beside the cot on which his son was dying, out in the mountains of the West, where he had been fighting for his life. The boy asked the father to pray for him, and the father had to tell him he could not do it. The boy knew too that once his father had been a faithful Christian man, the superintendent of the Sunday School, and always in his place at church. "Then," said his father, as he handed me the little Testament, "my son said, 'Well, if you cannot pray for your son, your son will pray for himself.' He put his pale hand into his pocket, and lifting this precious Book up, he offered a faithful prayer." The father had fallen upon his knees beside that cot in silent acceptance and condemnation. That boy had been won to God by a stranger who had sat beside him on the train. His card was in the little book, and I was glad to find he was one of my own personal friends. But that heartbroken, lone father said to me, and this is why I told you so tender a story, "A stranger had to step in and win my boy to Christ." With that word he fell to his knees in my office and found his place once more in the work of the Kingdom. Oh, these sacred friendships! Surely we will not waste them. Surely we will see the necessity of completing them, and making them Christian. I propose an honest campaign of our friends for Christ. Every Christian a center of evangelism in friendship. Grant us this, and there will set in among us at once the most overwhelming sweep of ingathered souls we have ever known.

"And he brought him to Jesus."

X

DIVINELY OUTMATCHED

But we see Jesus.—Heb. 2. 9.

THE remarkably far-reaching reasoning of
that text clause fairly leaped at my attention
recently as I was reading along this quite familiar passage of Scripture, of which it is so
eloquent a part. Somehow in my way of reading, I had never separated these four words in
their argument before. I had been reading the
whole passage. It was satisfactory as a passage.
The separation of the clause to attention came to
me as I put an emphasis, in reading it, upon the
first word. "We see Jesus" is in itself merely
a statement of fact. To be sure, it is a fact that
must be granted prime meaning. It is a fact
that has stirred poets and musicians. Some of
our loveliest songs have been written in the
desire

"To have seen His kind look when He said,
Let the little ones come unto me."

But that is not the power enclosed in this four-
word clause I have separated here for a text.
The man who wrote these words knew the chal-

lenge life was forever hurling at every man's faith. He was writing down a great liability in life, and then standing against it a sufficient faith. He was not merely seeking to construct a philosophy; he was declaring an experience. He had no exceptions to make in the test of his religion; he was simply underwriting everything that could come, with the confidence he had in his God.

The impressive, and to me startling meaning written here, lies in the introduction of the clause with the little connecting word "but." "But we see Jesus." There is in that the doggedness of ultimate victory. It overleaps all difficulty. It refuses to be discouraged. It would outmatch every hard thing with this great heaven-brought hope. "But," see who is for us! Yes, I know life is hard; you need bring me no argument there; I too am a man. I know sin is rampant. I know evil is strangely regnant. I know suffering is bitter. I know sorrow seems to hound the trail of all our joys. I know injustice is abroad. I know death is before us all. I know! I know! I know! "But we see Jesus."

Surely you see now with what defiant faith the author of Hebrews has written here this most heroic challenge. Surely, you see in this upleaping word how greatly he has caught for us the fact that God was in Jesus Christ out-

matching every human experience. Such words
as these write hope across all our lives, through
every experience we have thus far had, in blazing
defiance toward every experience that may
henceforth come.

Jesus Christ is the one great center of humanity in all its hopes and aspirations. O troubled
day of ours!—day to which so many distracting
ideas are being thrown, whatever you may work
out in your plans and purposes, and however
deep you may find yourself involved in mystery
and suffering, know this always: This Christ
of ours is everywhere and everywhen the Son of
God. God has matched him in the confidence of
his own plan against everything human sin
can ever come to mean. God doesn't experi-
ment. God doesn't guess. God never finds himself reduced to an alternative. He was sure
when he sent his Son to save the world. He is
sure now. We see darkly, but not so God.
Small-visioned men, who run impatiently about
with close-rimmed horizons drawn down before
them, may not know of the morning. But when
God matched Jesus against human sin, there
was then but one outcome possible. Jesus must
reign until he hath put all things under his
feet. All the world is marching to the corona-
tion of our Lord, and some wonderful day this
familiar old world of ours, which he has pur-

chased with his own blood, will own his sway, and he shall be Lord of lords, and the whole verse here, out of which I took the text clause, will be laid aside as accomplished history, back to which we can look through memories of some great strivings. "Now we see not yet all things put under him, but we see Jesus."

"But we see Jesus!" Hear it, out of the clamor of a world on which the human struggle against its hindrances is at times almost discouraging. This great word sings a quenchless hope. Christ is humanity's only chance. He is man's complete interpreter. We seem forever to catch in him the ever-luring intention God has in us. The author of Hebrews seems with this defiant word to stand squarely before the human story, and look with sure challenge along the way it is yet to proceed. He sees revealed beyond all the confusing strife that so easily blinds those who are in its midst the certain outcome of it all. I see man! Ah, what a sight! It brings blush of shame at times, and at times it brings fear, and at times it brings pride. There he goes, across so many centuries, trampling them out in bitterest sorrow. There he stumbles a poor sodden way in brutality and wasteful crime. There he sits in broken sorrow. I see man! But I see Jesus also! And I am very sure I have not seen the fact of this story of man, as it is sure to be

written at last, until I have actually seen above
it all the story of this Son of God. I do see him
too. It is such a meaningful fact for the world
now. It must take its place as an actual part
of our great civilization, a force undeniable in
the steady advance of every great movement.
You cannot look anywhere to-day and fail to see
this great dominating significance of our Divine
Master and Lord.

This is the sum of all true preaching; to effectually set the great truth of the overmatching
presence of the Son of God against everything
life can bring. If I could now utterly blot out
everything else, and drive directly to this great
truth; if I could but pin the attention of wearied
men and women, wearied often to the point of
discouraged surrender, and disclose there to
them this great sufficient fact; if I but knew how
to declare the beauty and the power, and the
sympathy, and the yearning of God as expressed
in his Son, and could make convincing to every
listener the fact that there is a great heart that
pities and a great peace that can be realized,
I would have found the realization of the preacher's commission. All of that to me stands
strongly forth in this text. See the world!
Look upon it with every complication you can
draw. There it lies, furrowed with graves as an
old man's face with wrinkled cares. Death!

Death! Death! The silent procession forever
filing down our street— dust to dust, earth to
earth, ashes to ashes. No one doubts it. This
strenuously living day heads for the grave. See
too the gloating ways of wickedness. How it
shoots at shining marks! Someone said once,
so all of us could say it often, "Death loves a
shining mark." But sin seems to love it more.
Death and a shining mark don't trouble me, as
do sin and a shining mark. How the devil
does love to throw the stain of sin across the
shining marks! The world is stained and
shamed—polluted by dishonesty, besotted by
intemperance, enslaved by passion. We are victims of flaming evil. And there are many folks
who, gazing upon such facts, draw desperation's
conclusion and say life is not worth living. Poor
discouraged Buddha knew nothing to do for
such a complicated sadness as life spread before
his eyes but to propose an eternal end of it all;
and he has been leading the millions of Christ-
less people he could reach, out to the darkness to
say, Leap now into the dark! Leap, hoping it
to be dark forever. That is the escape of Nir-
vana.

"But we see Jesus!" We stand to call to the
world everywhere to lift its eyes and see. Raise
your worn, wearied faces from your haunting
thoughts of evil and ruin, that have been stalk-

ing in terror along the pathway of man all his days. Look at man in the light of the presence of the Son of God. Know you that Jesus has given us a new human estimate. He has restated life. Never again shall we find our estimate of man in the broken image sin has made. Never again shall drunkard, and liar, and hypocrite and miser set the standard of our judgment. For we see Jesus! And seeing him we are to get the measure of God upon human life. Thereon we will read the estimate in manhood that makes it aware that its significance and interpretation are to be found not in the wickedness and wretchedness it may suffer, but rather, in the goodness and godliness it may attain. This, my friends, has come to be the firm basis of the confidence of Christianity. We take it and stand before every confounding situation life can present, and in answer to every difficulty interposed reply, "But we see Jesus."

1. I want us to take our stand beside the oft discouraging fact of human sin, and see what the overmatching fact of Jesus Christ will do for it. Sin is what breaks all our hearts, and sets us back upon ourselves with a downhearted judgment toward our race. Whenever we enter into any type of mechanical reform, and seek to bring about a high standard of living by the interposition of certain regulations, we find our-

selves complicated with the fact that unideal individuals make havoc with ideal laws. If man is ever to become the man he was meant to be, he must be saved from his sin. All the story of the ambition of our race, and of its tireless efforts toward its best life, can be traced in its struggle to free itself from its sin. We look back to-day from the comparatively, at least, proud place we occupy, in disgust at many of the things our ancient—and not very ancient either—ancestors tolerated, and pass our judgment upon them, only because we have attained the position where what we had approved yesterday has now come to be loathed. There can, however, be found but little permanence in a comfort that must be drawn in mere comparison. Our position to-day is a heartbreak to us all. This world as we know it is packed and crammed with misery. Sometimes the sins of men come so heavily upon our consciousness we feel broken before them. There are times when the reform of the world seems well-nigh hopeless. New tyrannies seem to come on to replace the old and worn or whipped-out troubles. Ancient wrongs seem once more to have found a new embodiment. Many the time the vision of sin's awful curse among us and upon us all has sent me from my pulpit back to my study, to bury my face in my impotent hands and cry to God for some new encouragement. Riot sends its shrill shriek through the troubled night. Drunkenness goes reeling its prohibited way among us, encouraged in its damnation by those who, because they fear they cannot arrest it, would wash their craven hands by licensing it. Brutal passion goes crushing its cruel, filthy way over the tender victims in its path, and gloats in its triumph as it leaves the blood-red trail of its foul presence in the tenderest places it can find among us. Yonder are wretched faces, smeared with gaudy colors, to hide the pale haunt of the absence of virtue. Yonder sits a broken-hearted mother looking across the cradle of a little loved one, into the darkness where wanders one just as dear.

There are no words we have yet been able to coin that will begin to tell what human life means, broken, and polluted, and ruined by sin. It may be familiar to our thoughts, but remains incapable of description. Crouching deep in all our own souls, as we are aware of the approaches it has made to our own lives, is the profound need we all feel, for the infinite forgiveness of God. Sin! Sin! Sin! We see a world crushed under its great cruel heel.

But! "But we see Jesus!" That is why I dwelt upon the fact as I did. That is why I dared call that discouraging list. Sin is divinely outmatched. That is the gospel. God has taken the field against Satan. Let not your hearts be troubled. Lift up your heads. Strengthen the feeble hands. Steady your trembling knees. The infinite hope of the gospel is drawn against the stormcloud of human sin.

I could easily fill all the time of all our sermons just telling the stories of this great overmatching fact of the Saviour from sin. I read every story of it I can find, and yet I know the finest stories are yet untold. *Twice Born Men,* and *More Twice Born Men,* will do for the titles of books as long as men can write, and the real story of every soul that has found the peace of pardon could well be given a place in the books, if men but knew how to write. I know a home where sin has written its most wretched story. It was on an alley, and housed as heroic a woman as ever refused to surrender her devotion and faith, before whatever sorrow beastly appetite could hang across her way. There in that little alley dwelling the weary but dauntless courage of that wife and mother stood beside the hot tub of suds, both day and night, in her determination to raise the family to the privileges the drunken father in the toils of selfish appetite refused to give them. She matched her not strong body against the sorrow. One bitter cold night I stood in that little home. In an old chair, close behind the stove, sprawled the drunken form of the man in deep sleep. The little ones had long been in bed. The noble woman said to me, as she choked her sobs, and brushed away the tears, "Mr. Rice, if I but had my own money, that I have earned with my hands in these tubs, which he has taken to spend on his own appetite, I could educate my children."

One wonderful day Mart met Jesus. It was sunrise in that little alley home. Never have I seen such a change in any life. He was a fine workman. His skill became at once efficient and dependable. The alley was deserted for a dwelling on the front street. The broken furniture was replaced with new and better pieces. New rugs found place on the floors. The tubs were set aside. Gladness found a dwelling place there. The father was a new man. The prison where for years he was so often an inmate became his place of ministering testimony. The church was the common center of the family's affection. Mart's testimony was standard evidence in the whole town of Christ's power to save. One unexpected day he was called upon to die, and he died as triumphant a death as could be accomplished, framing his very last breath into the words of a favorite hymn. The funeral was held from the church, and the services were attended by a crowd of people from every walk of life, as testimony to what Jesus

Christ had done with a sin-broken man. What think you of such a Saviour? One who can snatch a cursed bottle from a hating hand, and replace it with a tender loving ministry. One who can make of such a broken man a character of usefulness. I would lift that one case before you now, in order to find a way to say the same thing that could be said before a great host more, that in spite of everything sin hath wrought in this world, we still see Jesus. Not only do we behold him in cases of flagrant ruffians but we see him above every type of sin's distress: Jesus Christ, God's Son, our Saviour, sent here to outmatch whatever sin can do on this earth.

I wish it were possible in one continued discourse to follow the trail of this encouraging fact along the whole story of the outmatching efficiency of our Lord. There are still so very many things not yet overcome, and their yet parading presence in the earth puts comment on the lips of criticism of our religion. Our world is strewn with wrong. The Christian knows this as well as the infidel. While our patience is indeed tried, because we would with more rapid pace bring this world round to righteousness, we still hold fast our faith, and seek to keep firm step in the never retreating way that leads to God. We do see Jesus. But the whole wording out of which the text clause was wrenched reads, "We see him not yet with all things under his feet." But we see Him; and that is our assurance, and there hath been written also in the Book that he will yet put all enemies under his feet. The last enemy that shall be destroyed is death. So for our final stand in defiant faith now I want us to bring the assurance of this same contention in consideration of death.

2. Death! the unavoidable pit before every human path, "But we see Jesus." Cheer up, you death-bound world of men. Why go you mourning along your way? There is written for us, that we shall actually hold triumphant celebrations over death itself, and that we shall build a monument of life above the graves of this dying world. Death is only the final ravage of sin, striking back at the mortal body, to do in it that which it hath been forbidden to do to the soul. It is like a spiteful enemy turned out of a stronghold, whose going was made along a pathway of spite. I have seen it so. To all those who were near the battle lines, the sight of leaping flames, whose red hunger devoured whole towns the enemy had been compelled to leave, will not be easily forgotten. The retiring enemy would break the statuary, wreck the bridges, blow up the pavements, destroy the railroads. The trail of an enemy that has been turned out is an angry trail of scattered wreckage. But

though I were to tell you with vivid pictures the awfulness of such a fact, written with the hot hatred of all the wars that were ever fought, I could not begin to find an actual figure to tell the dreadful story sin has written in death, as it has been driven out of the human soul, and refused to leave without striking back in spite, with death, hideous death.

Let us not be deceived into a make-believe comfort, by thinking we have changed its real meaning by shifting its name, or denying reality. Let us look death straight in the face, and see what hope is written upon it. I cannot lift my eyes and miss its presence. The whole earth is honey-combed with graves. I have seen the sad procession in every land. It has always been true. The most impressive fact to the world traveler is the universal graveyard. From the gorgeous tombs of ancient kings in the valley at Luxor, into whose crumbling splendor a whole world's curiosity is now gazing, to the humblest hewn-out hole in the frozen ground of the northern settlers, death has left his common mark. It has struck our race down with heartlessness. It has gloated itself, as slow torture has crept up day by day, on tender lives. It has shouted in startling alarm as sudden call came. Death is here.

Do you dread death? Do you at times feel

the tremble of your own name written in black?
I saw the other day the account of a man who
read his own name in the death notices of the
city. It was meant for him too, and was not a
mere coincidence of two folks wearing the same
name. He went to look at the mistaken
announcement. Does such an incident grip your
own heart in meaning? Death has walked
through all our homes. It will walk there more.
Maybe we in the light carelessness of inex-
perience do not appreciate what death means.
But there is no hurry. The other day in my
church there stood upon the platform a most
beautiful group of little girls. They were the
dear little ones who were in the class that was
passing out of the Beginner's Department of our
Sunday school into the Primary Department.
They had to repeat in unison some Scripture
they had learned. Among other passages came
the twenty-third psalm. To hear those little
girls say those great words, whose meaning none
of them could even guess at (and we did not
want them to know either) made all our older
hearts tremble, and started tears on many a
more experienced face. One lovely little one
caught sight of some interested mother out there
in the audience, and as she fairly leaped on her
glad little toes, she waved her eager hand in
salutation and her little face glowed with gen-

uine joy as she repeated, "Yea, though I walk through the valley of the shadow of death, I will fear no evil." And we all laughed with her, and our laughter there was like a rainbow on the shoulders of a storm cloud. But we laughed. I went out from there to sit beside a dear old saint who had known Christian experience for many years. She had trailed it through sorrow and joy. She was coming up to the end of this world. She asked me to read to her that great psalm the little girl had laughed her way through. The comments of her trustful life upon the rich sentences as they fell from my lips, were precious to hear. She had learned them as a little girl. She had come to know them as a woman and a mother. She had come to trust them at the end. Death is before us.

"But we see Jesus!" Thank God! There he stands unafraid and triumphant before this bitter fact we dread. Victorious on the tomb's threshold. There is no stain on his garment. No sorrow clouds his brow. Two angels who have been specially designated to sit beside the deserted grave to inform those who come seeking the dead, that he has risen from the grave, wait there a while to tell it. Then his own word gets its clear meaning, "I am the resurrection, and the life: he that believeth in me, . . . shall never die." That is what we mean when we say we see Jesus beside death. The Christian grave is not a failure. It is no mere buoy to mark a reef whereon another wreck was made. The Christian grave has now come to be a goal obtained. The post where a race was won. The monument of an eternal victory. We do not tremble to speak of those who have left us.

> "When at last I near the shore,
> And the fearful breakers roar,
> 'Twixt me and the peaceful rest,
> Then while leaning on thy breast,
> May I hear thee say to me—
> Fear not! I will pilot thee."

We know death is before us. But we see Jesus. We are not afraid.

In all this we have so imperfectly said now we have but hinted at the real wonder of our theme. It runs far, across every exposure of life, to write this same sure divine outmatching truth against every trouble life can bring. Jesus Christ is God's answer to every wrong thing on this earth. We who believe him cannot doubt the outcome. He comprehends within himself a world's salvation. One great triumphant day we shall behold him in all that is noblest and most transcendent, in truth, in honor, in faith, in meekness, in humility—in all that human life can call for as it runs the whole gamut of its experience. All will be embraced in him; and lifting our sometimes tear-flushed, but then confident eyes we shall see Jesus, King of kings, Lord of lords, All in all, blessed forever. Till that fulfilling day I take my stand amid whatever life can raise against me. I would not deny it. But I see Jesus.

XI

ADORNING THE DOCTRINE

That they may adorn the doctrine of God our Saviour in all things.—Titus 2. 10.

THAT is one of the most searching passages of expectant Scripture I know. It has always put the sharp point of judgment into my life. I am uncomfortably conscious in its presence, of the high task to which I am set when I assume the responsibility of Christian profession. The commission of the Christian is difficult. He is charged with the positive measure of goodness. The mere negative interpretation of harmlessness is not sufficient. He must be good. His life must be ministrant in righteousness. This text puts it doubly difficult. A man, just any man, a common sort of a man such as I am, facing the uncertain things of a life that meets struggle every day; I must be so carefully adjusted in my actions and thoughts as to adorn the doctrine of God. Adorn it! I am not called to merely subscribe to this doctrine; nor am I told that I am not to injure the doctrine, nor hinder the progress of the doctrine. There is to be no mark of my success as a Christian given me because I simply kept the law, and was not convicted of having broken it. I am commissioned to adorn the doctrine. In me the doctrine itself is to have an attractive setting. In my life the gospel of Jesus Christ, my Saviour, is to be beautiful.

All this goes straight to the heart of individual conduct in interpretation of its responsibility. We will at once have difficulty with all that self-serving attitude which imagines it has covered itself with safety when it declares it can see no harm in this or that, hence this or that will be indulged. There is positive measure in Christian life. We cannot defend ourselves with negatives. It was a great leap in ideals when Jesus, after giving full recognition of the old commandments which were all framed about refusals, and based on what must not be done, added boldly the positive interpretation of them all to be, that we should love the Lord our God with all our heart, and our neighbor as ourselves. He had given us a working formula. The other was the very best that could be done with negatives, and it will never be repealed. But the world will never be brought under the subjection of a religion that deals in negatives, and will only be won by a gospel of positives. So the exhortation of our text presents a positive word for life shaping, and requires that we look steadily at it as men and women ready to be honest with life.

How is a man, just an ordinary man—for this must be a general commission—how is a man, beset with multitudinous foes, and stumbling along paths of difficulty familiar to us all; a man who blunders often even in his best purposes; how is the kind of a man we know ourselves to be, ever to be able to be set up as an adornment of Christian doctrine? I can easily understand how he can agree to it, and espouse it, and say, even as he stumbles, that it is the truth. But that is not the high calling to which we have been called. There seems here to be a direct commission to Christians to make beautiful the doctrines of our religion. The idea presents a difficulty. Not only is this difficult because the thing to be adorned is in itself supremely beautiful, but it is doubly difficult because it presents two distinct expressions neither of which is in relation. A doctrine is abstract; whatever I can bring to it in life is concrete. How shall I combine them? I have read well-written articles on "Making the Home Beautiful"; and the propositions made were all illustrated with the attendant designs,—rugs, and pictures, and draperies, and lawns and hedges. But I have never read an article, nor have I ever seen any illustrations of how to adorn a doctrine. It seems the word "adorn" has gotten out of its zone. I wonder if that is not one of the serious handicaps religion carries when endeavoring to reach folks. It is hard to translate the abstract into the concrete terms we more quickly understand. If I am to think close beside the men and women about me in religious terms, I must clothe my doctrines in concrete form, and stand Christianity in Christian living as an evangelistic appeal. The doctrine must become incarnate. It must live beside men, labor in familiar fields, endure the trials we all know, and shout in triumph with us. The doctrine must become a life. Put principle in flesh and blood, and you will have adorned principle. Live a human life, clothing the doctrine of God our Saviour in an actual person, and you will have made it beautiful.

To adorn the doctrine therefore, I contend, is to exemplify it. In the pioneer process of learning, a clear demonstration is a primary essential. Fundamental education is based to-day largely on illustration. To translate declarations into concrete facts is the teacher's first art. You cannot make words any more than words, without it. The vast improvements in school books of to-day over yesterday are not evident in the superior facts they are imparting, but, rather, in the fine illustration of the same old facts our fathers and mothers had to learn in a duller way. Suppose you should set yourself to impart to a child the knowledge of red. That child never having seen the brilliant color, you were left with every possible knowledge, and a great vocabulary, to make clear to the eager mind that consciousness which now possesses you when you hear the familiar little word. How would you tell him red? You would start out with a blunt declaration that could not be disputed in its basal truth and say, "Red is red"; and the child would agree with you because red could not be anything else if it was red. The limitation of your demonstration would, however, seek relief in your knowledge, as you enlarged such a declaration with the statement, "Red is the seventh color in the spectrum, my son"; and the complicated situation would reveal nothing to the child. Then you would turn to the chemical explanation which entered into all the red pigment yet known. Suddenly your troubled way cleared, and you thought of some information that would make the color an analyzed fact for his consciousness to grasp. "My son, light can be made to vibrate, and as the vibrations increase we obtain the whole gamut of the spectrum. Of course what colors lie concealed at both ends of the visible ones, we designate by the word we learned in our physics, v-i-b-g-y-o-r, we do not know. But when the light wave begins to vibrate at the rate of three hundred and ninety-

six to four hundred and seventy trillion times
a second, we have red." And having made such
a scientific statement you thought, of course,
the child could just see the color, but there was
even more confusion on his face than before;
and what at first he had thought was but a
simple matter, "red is red," he began to believe
was the most non-understandable matter that
had ever been hinted to him. Just at that point
the janitor, having heard all the abstract argument, brought in a pot of red paint, and with
a brush splashed a gleaming streak across the
wall, and said, "That, my lad, is red!" and with
one stroke of demonstration had been accomplished what all scientific reasoning would have
been unable to clear. I saw a class of children
in school with a teacher who knew her art. Each
little pupil had a box of yellow corn on his desk.
The lesson was "ten." They placed ten kernels
of corn in a row, and counted them in unison.
Then on each row the last kernel was pushed up
alone above the others. "Count the row again,"
said the teacher. They counted to nine, and the
teacher, pointing to the separated grain, said
quickly, "Plus one equals ten." Every child saw
it at once, and immediately was ready to tell
a story about "ten," the first one being an eloquent one, thus: "If I had nine bananas and
some one would give me one more banana, I

would have ten bananas." That was adorning ten so it will never again be a mere abstract word to those children. Adorn the doctrine! Great principle in Christian dynamics.

Here lies the burden of our living. Here rests the heavy responsibility attendant upon what the Christian says and does. We dare not be careless with life. There is no measure so severe in its exaction as that which is upon us who dare the name of Christian, to adorn the doctrine of God. The text was spoken directly to some slaves who were exhorted to make Christianity beautiful and attractive to their masters, by the lives they lived as slaves, their masters being heathen. It is the same thing Jesus meant when he said, "Let your light so shine." The meaning is in the word "so." It is the variable term. When Jesus spoke thus he likely pointed to a little clay lamp with a sputtering wick of hemp in it. The word "so" meant the best light they had. To-day the same exhortation stands beside the greatest searchlight and demanding all we can be, says, "So shine!" The "so" of Jesus, for his people's expectation, keeps up with the very best. Even so this word "adorn," of our text keeps abreast of the day. The adornment of yesterday may have done then, but it will not do for to-day; and the requirement of Christian life to-day in adorning the doctrine of God our

Saviour must keep up with adornment as interpreted in the last acceptance. Christianity is not written in stationary terms that are fixed in any age; it is just as progressive as mankind can become. The commission of adorning the doctrine will, with every new age's interpretation of adornment, stand clear as obligated up to the last and highest measure of what adorning means. There are some kindred passages in the Word that must now be put beside this interpretation I have made—"Holding forth the truth in beauty." "That ye may be blameless and harmless, the sons of God, without rebuke, in the midst of a crooked and perverse nation, among whom ye shine as lights in the world; holding forth the word of life; that I may rejoice in the day of Christ, that I have not run in vain, neither labored in vain."

Whatever any of us may think about the perplexing problems that to-day are striking with such fierceness at the heart of purity and goodness, the fact does stand clear that there never was a day when mankind in general stood as high as it stands to-day. I do not say this, blinded at all to the big menacing evils that seem to have such a grip on our present civilization. I cannot be dull to the fact that much we brand as evil and outlawed to-day is so because of our higher standards, which in a lower yes-

terday we never noticed. Many men yet live
who can testify to conditions when they were
boys which would not be tolerated anywhere
to-day. In the night you can only with difficulty
discern the general outline of the bulking mountain against the sky. As the fuller light of
approaching day filters through the opening
shutters of dawn, the more rugged lines of the
hills become visible, and you can mark where
the great rocks stand. When the sun has leaped
from the goldened east you can easily see the
tall, ragged pines that stand against the sky.
Under the flooding of the noontime you can see
the great glistening eagle as he wheels his stately
circles about the crags. You must, however,
catch a direct, penciling ray of brilliant sunshine in order to see the flying particles of dust
in the very air you have been breathing and had
not known it was all the time well-nigh choking
with its pollution. As a great human race we
are climbing laboriously, and heroically too I
am sure, toward the perfect day. I know how
badly we have stumbled and have even fallen
prostrate at times. Once in the darkness we
saw only the mountain's contour. In the figure
of the morning I just used I am not just able to
tell where we stand. Perhaps we are where
we can make out the pines along the rough horizon ahead. Anyhow, there are many things in

public life to-day we are prosecuting and condemning, that yesterday we at least tolerated. But wherever we are in the application of the comparison, the Christians are there to make sure to adorn the gospel. We are in the midst of our day, whatever that day does, to make beautiful the doctrine of God our Saviour. Never was there a day when conduct was so carefully examined and so keenly judged as this day. There are many things before our civilization which are provoking comment, and about which the Christian cannot be uncertain. Things that one day did not compel anyone to have any opinion on we find ourselves as Christians to-day compelled to hold the right opinion on. Never before as to-day has it been so hard to adorn doctrine. Lesser days than these offered easier distinction. Telemachus could leap into a mad arena before bloodthirsty thousands, and in noble protest at the strife write his name with fame forever, by the practice of what to-day our whole civilization practices. May God grant that the millions whose lives were crushed in bleeding trenches may do for accursed war what the lone figure of that sacrificed monk did for gladiatorial combat. Adorn the doctrine! Catch the commission to-day! We can no longer merely stand amid the general condition of the crowd. We must stand out peculiar. We must be superior in motives. We must win for our cause by the strong beauty of our lives. It is the divine conscription of Christianity that religion be given the supreme place in life, "the high calling in Christ Jesus." The world well knows the motto written across the human story in the dearly bought blood of the Son of God, who never flinched at the price. Can we meet the test laid against us by our text before such facts as stare at us from every page of the story of our faith? It little becomes any of us before such a call to talk much about excuses for doing things which at least tend to weaken our influence. I ask in shameful consciousness of the painful littleness of my own influence, is my life such that anyone anywhere would ever think the doctrine I profess is more beautiful because of me? Character analysts are all about us. They disclose our influence on every hand. Someone with keen ear heard some word I spoke, and told it. Someone with keen eye saw some deed that fell carelessly from my hand, and told it. Someone with keen nerve felt some act I committed, and told it. My whole character was weighed and exposed. But though difficult the judgment we all meet, I believe we have provision made, whereby we shall be able to bear it. Our doctrine is indeed sublime. But it never does look so sublime as when clothed

in a true human life. Who can tell in words the
wonderful story of God's great good man Job?
The Bible has the very best that words can do,
but we feel there is yet so much more in Job.
Cast down, but not discouraged. Laughed at,
but never wavering. Tempted and tried, even to
the last throw of pain the devil could devise
this side death, but never faltering. Job, God's
great servant, suffering, but without a single
doubt! How does he adorn the doctrine of God
across the centuries! See the noble mother
beside whom I stood the other day as she looked
into the deep darkness of the grave of her only
child. Yesterday, only yesterday, no home in
all the land was more content and glad; to-day
she stands in the unmeasured anguish of her
loss, and you might think there would be heard
some words of complaint or criticism. But she
is a Christian. From the thin quivering lips are
breathed those great far-reaching words which
have reached through the gloom so often, and
held fast the faith, "The Lord gave and the Lord
hath taken away. Blessed be the name of the
Lord." Good was this sorrow for us all. The
doctrine of divine sovereignty has been adorned
and made a reality there. This is the story of
faithful Christian living all across the ages.
Even now Jesus Christ in glory is twining about
some lovely crowns, immortal garlands to be

worn by those who to-day endure, but adorn in endurance. Thank God, here and now, for the beautiful souls sometimes wrapped in shattered bodies, sometimes placed on uncertain feet, and ministering with palsied hands, and clad in tattered garments of poverty, but souls that breathe the breath of truth, and make real and beautiful in their places the very truth of Christ. We have all seen them. We know their street addresses even now. Souls who lay without falter on God's altar of sacrifice, all they have, even their poor tortured bodies, and never allow a murmur to pass their lips. Thank God for great beautiful human life. Beautiful in spite of that sometimes strange dispensation evident in this world. Beautiful even in earth's poverty. Beautiful though the fine chisels of culture may never have been set to heighten the brow, and shape refinement on the face. Beautiful, whatever the world hangs round it, for God is working on it, and he has set the marks of loveliness upon that face.

We have not been studying now a passage clothed in a mysterious something that forever remains beyond our reach. "We are his workmanship." We have therefore upon us the judgment of an expecting world. Ours is indeed the high calling. We are only men and women, but we dare not be any less than men and women led by the spirit of our Saviour. There is no higher honor available to mankind than that which lies in the line of our Christian commission. I care not for the laurels of the conqueror whose name is writ in the heroic blood of men who had to die to get such honors. Our honor, until the great change shall come, may be detected in the weeping eye, the aching head, the wounded spirit, the breaking heart, if only thereby we may but be able to honor our God and magnify the doctrine of his salvation among men.

XII

YOUR BOY

"The father's life is bound up in the lad's life."—Gen. 44. 30.

THE simple phrasing of that sentence text out of the very earliest part of the Bible, and across long centuries of human experience, is tender and beautiful, and yet powerful, and carrying to-day as much meaning for all our homes as it did in the home of the early patriarch. When once it is separated thus to attention it will not easily be shaken from memory. It is a great verse for fathers to read. It expresses in convincing manner a fine feeling we have always had, of the real relationship of a father to his son, and at the same time carries a keen condemnation for the painful lack of its practice in so many of our lives.

I chose this text out of the pathetic appeal made by Judah, the eldest son of Jacob, to his unknown brother Joseph, whom he had sold in bondage many years before, and who had after most thrilling experience climbed his way from slavery and prison, up to the highest place in the nation beneath the king. Joseph had instituted a fine bit of strategy, and placed all his brothers before him in apparent dishonesty, a dishonesty it would seem even with proffered charity. The feeling was so very tense at one time that Joseph had to leave the room, and wash his face, for the reason he could not longer restrain his tears before his brethren. To me one of the most humanly expressive verses in all the Old Testament is a phrase about Joseph saying, "And he washed his face and went out." Trapped in the well laid plan his brethren stood helpless. The specific blame had fallen upon the youngest brother, who had been brought on this second journey of relief against the protest of his aged and infirm father. Joseph had now demanded that he be left as a bondman to obtain release of the others. I do not know of a finer drawn, and more tragic incident worked out in human life than that. It carries all the elements of a fascinating story.

The text clause is the point of climax in the very fine speech made by Judah, offering himself as a substitute for Benjamin, for he was already surety to the anxious father for the lad's safety. It had been necessary before Jacob, keenly remembering the tragic loss of his other son across the years, would allow Benjamin to be taken on the long journey to Egypt, for Judah to declare to him, "If I bring him not unto thee, . . . then, let me bear the blame forever."

The memory of wonderful years waited upon Joseph's mind as he listened to the appeal. How he, a young lad, had been planfully disposed of by cruel jealousy. He never could forget that muddy old pit, into which they hurled him thinking at first he could be left there to die. Then the better plans of this same Judah prevailed, and the sentence was changed, and that tender dumfounded boy was taken away by some Midianites, to be sold a slave in a distant country. He can now see again that huddling company of hating brothers as they divided the money they got for him as he rode away heart-broken and chagrined. Once more Judah is pleading for a change of sentence. "I pray thee, let thy servant abide instead of the lad a bondman to my lord; and let the lad go up with his brethren. For how shall I go up to my father, and the lad be not with me?"

You cannot read this chapter and restrain the tears of sincere appreciation for the sacred affection of that father. It is the pulse of the whole story. "The father's life is bound up in the lad's life." Sacred situation! Sacred for both father and son. A situation which is most certain to work safety for each. Across all the years, no finer suggestion has ever been made with which to face the so-called boy problem.

Thank God for the man who can wrap him-

self about the life of his boy effectually. I
thank God, and take courage for every boy whose
father is actually wrapped about him. Each
thus finds safety in the other. I wish it were
the universal testimony of fatherhood. I wish
no boy had ever been failed there. The failure,
however, at this vital relationship is a growing
danger of our day. One of the most impressive
and successful men, it has ever been my privilege to call a friend, said to me one day, as we
were discussing the boy problem, "The only real
great gift any man can make his boy is himself."
I am perfectly sure of the truth of that word.
It is so easy to write a check. It is so easy to
send him away for a trip. It is so easy to give
a boy anything else than the very gift he needs
most from his father. "The father's life is bound
up in the lad's life." Fortunate lad that. Sen-
sible father that.

This is a direct call to the preservation of
home influences. This tender and effective relationship is not a matter to be accomplished
under the unnatural conditions that obtain in
every other association. It is only under the
true life of home the lad will ever come under
the intimate influence of his father. I wish I
might say that into attention in this day when
so many influences are removing from all of
us those strong molding forces which home alone

can mean to human relationships. I believe I am familiar with all the easily made arguments appealing to the father's place as counsel and chum for work and play. I am sure I appreciate the full force of those arguments. I believe in all they can mean. I am, however, convinced over and beyond them all, that nowhere do we need the real application of the influence of the father upon his son as we need it in the ordinary life of the home. It carries primary strength there, because it is natural. When a father plays the game of his boy, there is a consciousness that it is put on, and not natural. He is out of date in games, no matter how well he holds his interest. Even the most ordinary games have been changed so much that rules the father played by are laughed at by his boy. I took my father to see a game of baseball when I was a college ball player. He was disgusted with our pitcher because he threw the ball so no one could hit it. He said when he played ball the pitcher was a man who was in the game to throw the ball for the purpose of being hit. Any boy of to-day will know what an up-to-date comment that is on the game. No matter how well the father may play, however, and however commendable the act may be for him to endeavor to play his boy's games, he is bound to a comparison in that game as unnatural.

Home is that father's natural chance. There whatever he does, must be forever measured in the realm of his own responsibility, and mistakes there are calamities. The problem which is so constantly presenting itself in every home where growing boys are found, is a problem relating to the loneness of the boy's soul. He wants someone who can honestly listen to him. The problem attendant upon that serious fact is not material but human. It is the genuine association of soul and life that will solve that problem. I remember somewhere in my reading to have seen the description of the home of an old apple-woman in Paris. All the material equipment she possessed was the little fruitstand, with a great umbrella raised above it. Every evening she gathered there her family of children in the perfect bondage of love. That little description has abided with me through years. The power of the home is not in its rugs, or its hangings, or its conveniences, but in its spirit. In spite of the absence of equipment there have been well nigh perfect homes, and, assisted by every equipment luxury could conceive, utter wreck of home life has been made. "The father's life is bound up in the lad's life," that will meet the trouble which seems to-day to be the agreed problem everywhere, the much discussed boy problem. It must be primarily solved by the father in the home. It may yet require us to raise up a whole generation of new fathers, with a deep sense of their indebtedness to their greatest task in this world, that will interpret lodge and club always after their prior claim at home.

Your boy is taking on every day his cargo of character, to set sail upon the sea of life from the port of his home. From the portals of your hearthstone may sail away a whole wonderful fleet. With them, you, sir, are to make register upon life's to-morrow. There is nothing that so awes a man, who is a man, as the big fact once actually facing him, of the propagation of an immortal soul through him. Let him first look into his own infant's face, and behold how strangely different that little one is from all others. Let him catch there, in the glint of that newly opened eye in this world, the spark immortal which was kindled from the torch intrusted to him; a spark he could kindle but can never quench. When once the sense of father-hood dawns fully upon a man's mind, it will stun him with responsibility—that strange sense of Deity which a father seems to express to his child, and which his very name stands first for in the multiplying words that lad shall learn. God forgive all of us for the shortcomings we have all brought to this great responsibility. I found a little sentence recently in some new-made

ritual, composed by a minister for his own use
in the service of baptism of infants. It charges
the parent with the solemn fact, that the first
thoughts that child will ever have about God
are thoughts he will have about his parents. I
have been putting that fact into the service every
time I have rendered it since seeing the sentence. It startled me. I called the word to the
bar of my own experience, and I found the earliest words expressive of God in my own life,
and the very facts of his relationships to me that
have grown stronger with the years, to be those
things which bloomed in my own home beside
my beloved father and mother. No one had ever
hinted to me before, however, the fact which
now I see, that one day I would, as a father,
actually stand for God to another, and a confid-
ing life, who would be taught at the altar of my
home and look up to God and say "Father."
What did he know of what the word "father"
meant? Nothing but what it meant in me to
him. That to me is the most overwhelming
interpretation of my fatherhood, as I look into
my child's face, that has ever seized my soul.
It is the sacred burden of fatherhood. We talk
much about the boy problem. It has a regular
place in almost every religious convention. I
am convinced, and after thought enough upon it
to satisfy me of my conviction, am ready to say,

that the so-called boy problem is all a misnomer. It is a father problem. The problem of your boy, sir, is very largely wrapped up in you. The only hopeful approach to the solution of whatever the problem is, is from the father side of it.

There is an opportune time in every boy's life when the hero of all heroes on earth is that boy's father. It is a serious, an almost irreparable blunder, if for any reason the boy shall be disappointed in that expectation. You will easily remember some little impression which at that moment was made upon your ready life. Out of that crucial period to me comes a simple memory which I know was never so much as remembered beyond the passing moment, by my hero. A little group of small children had been unable to drive away from our playground an old white cow, whose presence scared us all. We had thrown tiny pebbles toward her, but none of even these flew far enough to even touch her. My father came by. We appealed. I can see to this day the flashing red trail of that flying brick, and hear the big, delicious sounding thud, as it struck her old white side, and see the vanishing presence of that menace to our pleasure. Of course I know now it is true my father actually did throw with a few unnecessary whirls of his arm that would have made us laugh in later years. But at that moment he was the hero physical of all men on earth to me. If any father will successfully give himself to his boy at that period of his life, he can put indelible impress upon him, and the confidence of the lad will put also most powerful impress upon the father, for this is mutual business we are at.

The problem of your boy is in you. When a man came to me in genuine and deep concern about his young son, and asked me to have a talk with the lad because he had become addicted to the use of profanity, I did not hesitate a moment, because I knew the situation. I said as I looked that father straight in the eyes, "No, sir! I will never talk to your son on the question of profanity while his father swears as he does. I am, however, ready right now to talk with his father about the sin his son has gone staggering into." As the tears broke from his honestly concerned eyes, he bowed his head and said, "I guess you are right." How can teaching and preaching break through the example of fatherhood? The boy problem I insist is the father problem.

There are so many things about this wonderful age of ours that easily stir our sense of appreciation that we are in danger of failing to note the failures which sometimes are allowed to slouch along in the overemphasis of other matters that savor of victory. I am concerned over the neglect of home nurture. Fatherhood is monopolized by business. Business is the chief expression the men of our age are making. Never have they found such strong and world impressive privilege in business as now. The tides of every nation and the throb of all the peoples of the earth seem to be felt at the door of the great modern office. Manhood is interested. Men endeavor to excuse the neglect of anything and everything else, by an argument that if they provide for their families they have certainly done their duty there; and they are willing even to set a more lavish measure to what that duty shall enjoin from them, than any men have ever felt before. But, after all, it must be reduced, in the last analysis, to merely mean groceries, shoes, clothes, school, and a dash of pleasure. Fathers are losing themselves to their boys in the consuming passion to make a success of this world. They seem oft mindless of the fact, that at the same time they are losing themselves to everything else, in order to accumulate a fortune to leave to their children, the very objects of their affection are starving and being unfitted to receive what is being gathered for them, for the painful reason that they are being deprived of the much higher contribution of their fathers' life. Boys want their fathers, not their fathers' money. They can make money. A boy who is not capable of taking care of himself in the world as it is to-day, if his father will do his fatherly duty by him when a boy, would make an utter wreck of an endowment if it were given him.

There is an eloquent man abroad to-day—and he is legion—who comments enthusiastically upon every suggestion of a home problem, and declares, as though the final deduction had at last been drawn, "A woman's sphere is in the home." When he has delivered himself of this great conclusion he imagines the blame of all failure in the home is thenceforth lodged in its proper place. The mother must carry the burden of home failure. I am weary of that old threadbare misstatement. The mother, God bless her, let all the world thank God for what she has done; but that mother with fair opportunity will hold her girl. But what of the lad? I believe I know somewhat of the power of a mother's devotion. I have seen it in its undeniable persistence. I know it will never die from a boy's life. I know how a mother fastens herself to the very soul of her son, and that all the debris a life of sin can heap upon him, cannot obscure that undying influence. God pity the boy whose mother may have failed him. I

heard Judge Lindsey tell a story one night several years ago, and among the many heart-
gripping stories I have heard him tell, this one
has held strongest to me. It was an incident
that had come before his court for care. A
ragged little fellow was often brought before
the Judge for truancy from school. It seemed
that no punishment the teachers could devise
had any reform influence, and even in spite of
the constant injunctions from the court Tim
would skip school and get some job and work.
One day in reproving him the Judge said, "Now,
Tim, there will be time enough for you to work
when you become a man." The little fellow
replied like a flash: "My father was a man,
and he didn't work. He went off and left mother
and me, and I guess that's what killed her, too."
Finally after continually breaking every instruction, Tim appeared in court one day of his own
accord, and upon his face shone a new expression. There was a blaze of confidence in his eyes.
Walking up to the Judge, he pulled from his
pocket a dirty, crumpled piece of paper, and
handed it up for inspection, saying as he did so,
"I'm going to remember now, all the things you
have told me, Judge, and I am going to school
regular now, for I've got that job all done!" He
stood back to await the Judge's inspection of
the crumpled paper he was carefully unfolding.

It was read with increasing interest. It was a receipted bill. Every little deposit that had been made was entered on the bill. Sometimes the amounts were but odd pennies. That little ragged, criticized, pursued fellow had actually paid with pennies and nickels the full price of fifty dollars for a little headstone for his mother's grave.

"My boy," said the Judge, "is this what you have been doing while you have been missing school so much?"

And Tim answered as he wiped some tears from his dirty, but manly cheeks: "I wanted her to have a monument too, Judge, like the others. She's done a lot for me. That's all I can do now for her."

Oh, yes, I know how wonderfully well a mother can do for a boy, but it is unfair to make it so hard for her to succeed at it. Work as she will, and urge as she may, your boy is quick to note to that urging mother, that the manhood of his father finds little expression in the church! And you need not wonder when you see signs of the breaking away of the ideas he has had toward Christian manhood, and in less time than you can believe, he has gone headlong, breaking every restraint, and plunging into ruin. The evident reason is that unlike the old patriarch so beautifully phrased by our text, your life has not been wrapped up in the life of your lad.

Men, I am asking you, because of the uneven battle for the family which is so often cast upon the faithful godly mother; you who occupy, not only the powerful place called fatherhood, but you who add to that the responsibility of being the molders of the public expression of the day, what can be said that will win the passion of to-day's manhood to this great task? The history of to-morrow is being made ready to-day. The only effectual way to write history is before it is made. The mere historian who tells the story of what has been is but a reporter. The historian who writes it by dictation of the lives of those who are to make that history to-morrow is the truest historian. We cannot afford to sacrifice our sons on low and unworthy altars. Your boy, sir, is an issue in you to-day. Greece died because the men who builded her glory were sacrificed on bleeding fields of battle, and left no sons to take their places. The Greek of to-day has not sprung from the loins of Leonidas and Miltiades. The most staggering blow the terrible war, through which our world has just staggered its way, has struck at this old world can never be reckoned here. Out there across the sodden fields of Europe lie millions and millions of the world's best young sons, and they have left no sons in their places. You fathers, of this doubly expected day, must not fail to carry well the responsibility of what your fatherhood means, even unto the extreme of consecrated passion. Fathers, I appeal to you. I appeal to you for the family. I appeal to you for family religion. I appeal to you for your boy. Be fair with your responsibility. Be fair for the church's sake. Be fair for your nation's sake. Be fair for your boy's sake. Be fair for Christ's sake. I appeal to you fathers for your boys.

Seldom have I ever read an incident that insisted on its own application in my conduct so, as one I saw somewhere in my reading, as recorded in the experience of Doctor Myers, of Boston. He said he became acquainted with the ship surgeon of one of the large liners crossing the Atlantic. The surgeon told him as they were talking one day, that on the voyage he had just then completed, a boy fell overboard just before the ship was to sail. The crew with their systematic drill had hastened to attempt the rescue. The lad was pulled on deck, and, according to all the rules for restoring one who has been drowned, they did their best. They stripped off his outer garments, they turned his body over a few times, worked his arms in an endeavor to start lung action, and in every way they knew, they sought to restore the boy to

life. After they had done their best, they were
to make report to the chief surgeon, who had
merely been a spectator from a point of advantage some distance away. The surgeon said he
came down to pass upon the incident, and see in
a mere routine manner if there was anything he
could do. The one in charge of the matter
reported the lad to be beyond all assistance.
The surgeon said he just felt impelled to go
personally to the little stark body, and see if
everything had been done, and as he looked into
the white face for the first time he discovered
it was the face of his own boy. No longer could
he agree, or even imagine that all had been done
that could be done. He snatched his coat from
his shoulders, and fell upon his knees beside the
body of the lad he loved. He blew into his
nostrils. He breathed into his mouth. He
turned him over, and over, and over again. He
simply begged God to bring that boy back again.
For four, long, terrible hours, that father surgeon worked over him, and just as the sun was
going down the first flutter of breath was
detected that gave evidence the boy was yet
alive. Then the great doctor said: "Now with
my boy mine again, I declare I will never see
another boy drown, without taking off my coat in
the first instant, and doing for him everything
I can do unto the last extreme of my strength,

just as I would if I knew he were my own boy."
Surely, such a story as that will strike home to
every father's heart with its irresistible meaning.   The passion we may feel in somewhat more
peculiar force toward our own, should leap in
true measure to inspire our true fatherhood
toward every boy's interest.   The problem of
your boy is the problem of every boy, and as you
do your highest duty by your own, you will
thereby best fit yourself to do your highest duty
by every other boy.

Let me close these words with a poem by my
personal friend, Edgar Guest, who is working
every day practically at the task in his own
home, and sentimentally throughout the whole
world with the fine fatherly interpretation he
puts into the home:

> "I have seed to raise, and I plow the field,
>   And I plant my crops with care,
> And I thank the Lord for the rain he sends,
>   As I watch them growing there.

> "But I don't sit down with a book by day,
>   And let my fields run wild;
> For crops won't grow by themselves I know;
>   Is it different with a child?

> "I've a boy to raise, and I want a man,
>   When his growing days are done;
> And a man must work for the crop he seeks;
>   Is it different with a son?

"Will strangers care for my wheat out there,
    When the weeds grow rank and wild?
If my crop would shrink if I idled here,
    Dare I idle with my child?

"Yes, I'll work for him, and I'll play for him,
    And I'll do the best I can,
For the Lord has given me a son to raise,
    And I want to raise a man.

"Yes, my eyes are set on the harvest years,
    When the long, hard task is done;
So I'll pull the weeds from his life myself,
    For I dare not shirk my son."[1]

---

[1]Used by permission of Reilly & Lee Co., owners of copyright, Chicago.